In the Valley of Decision

Insights to Sustain Your Faith

Roosevelt Dunn

COLORADO SPRINGS, COLORADO

First printing 2007

ISBN-13: 978-1-934038-00-0
ISBN-10: 1-934038-00-8
LCCN 2006933148

This book is dedicated to my wife, Emma,
who for forty-eight years has remained
by my side through the thick and thin.
Also, to my children, Dad loves you.

Table of Contents

Section Four: Preparing for His Return

Section Five: Q&A on Finances and Marriage

Preface

IN JUST A SHORT amount of time we have taken a unique opportunity to capture in print one of the most profound Servants of God—Pastor Roosevelt Dunn. His revelation in scripture is one-of-a-kind and we believe the collections contained within this book will *enlighten, restore and revitalize* your faith as you take the opportunity to meditate on the wisdom and timeless insights for daily living contained herein.

This book is practical for nearly all applications in our lives—marriage and family, single, poor and rich, healthy and sick, financially challenged, and the young and old. Regardless of where you are in life, you will eventually come upon a valley where you will be required to make a decision based on your faith in God and without any supporting feeling or affirmation from your closest family/friends. At such a critical time in life, *In The Valley of Decision*, will prove to be your most helpful resource for keying in on the will of God for you.

Be Blessed.

Earnest M. Dunn
Decision Time Publishing

Acknowledgments

AS ONE COULD IMAGINE, this project involved many contributors without whose involvement the task would have been impossible. This collection of devotionals has blessed each of us as we completed our part in putting this book together. We thank God for Pastor Roosevelt Dunn who allowed the Lord to speak through him and whose vision and leadership have taken us to greater levels in the ministry. Thank you to the editors: Takeitha Peterson, Sara Schleske, and Michelle Wills-Hill. As well, we thank the transcribers of the Pastor's messages: Jesse Harding, Michelle Williams and Margaret Will. Your time and effort on this behalf is sincerely appreciated. A special note of thanks is extended to Vickie Rhodes who has kept us all on task by handling the paperwork. Most of us would not have been able to work on the project had it not been for our understanding and supportive families. So, a special thank you and words of appreciation to the wives, husbands and children of this staff. Your love, patience and encouragement have given us the courage to move forward knowing you were there for us. And, finally, and highly important, we extend sincere appreciation to the Israelite Church of God in Christ family. Thank you for your prayers and words of encouragement.

It is our prayer and that you, the reader, will be blessed and inspired while reading this collection of devotionals and that you will share them with others, as the Lord leads.

Section One

A New Beginning

In the Valley of . . .

Spiritual Blindness

But if our gospel be hid, it is hid to them that are lost: In whom the god of this world hath blinded the minds of them which believe not, lest the light of the glorious gospel of Christ, who is the image of God, should shine unto them.

II Corinthians 4:3–4

Identifying Your Blindness

DID YOU KNOW THAT the god of this world has the ability to blind your mind? Some people refuse to believe that the Devil has this power. But he does. He will do all he can to blindfold, hinder, and even stop you from believing and receiving the Word of God.

It is his job to prevent you from receiving what God has promised you. It is his desire to keep you from becoming a recipient of all of God's blessings. Whether you choose to believe it or not, understand that Satan possesses specific powers and abilities.

Satan has blinded the minds of many believers; those who know the Word and act in accordance by Faith and those who know that Word and never act in accordance by Faith. He is yet after those believers who do not make time to understand the promises of God and obey His Word.

The scripture says, "*And ye shall know the truth, and the truth shall make you free.*" **John 8:32** But, it is only the truth that you know that will free you. It is only the truth that you have the ability to understand and that you can act upon. This truth is not hard. We are just blind to the victory that God has provided through His Son, Jesus Christ. Our mind can be blind to success, health, life and peace. All of these are promises that God has provided to us in His Word.

Satan is searching for the prayer-less person who does not know God. The person who complains and refuses to read the Word is whom he is searching for. Those individuals who are not faithful are his prey. Satan will attempt to stop us from doing everything that God has commanded us to do to become stronger and receive His unlimited blessings. Satan loves those who make excuses.

Uncovering the Blindfold

The statutes of the Lord are right, rejoicing the heart: the commandment of the Lord is pure, enlightening the eyes.

Psalms 19:8

Everyone of us is blind to a certain extent when it comes to spiritual things. "While we have light" we must "believe in the light, that we may be the children of the light." ***John 12:36*** There is not any among us who knows everything. This means right now you and I are blind to some things that God has promised us. This is why we have to pray, study the Word of God, and open our hearts so that more of God's light will come into us.

> When we allow God to penetrate our being, spiritual blindness is totally eliminated.

Find out what God requires and then ask Him for strength to do it. Ask God for knowledge to do what is necessary to be blessed. Once we really become associated with God and understand how He operates, we are on our way to being blessed. Develop a relationship with God. Let Him use you, and then, He will bless you. Open your eyes and understanding to the reality of God. Don't be the person who is, "ever learning, and never able to come to the knowledge of the truth." ***II Timothy 3:7***

Seeing Your Victory

When the eyes of our understanding are opened, sometimes we respond by saying, "I never saw it like that. All of this time, I did not know that I could have all of this." Success. Health. Life. Peace. When the blinders are removed, we recognize that we do not have to wait to be healed. We confess *now* that we are already healed. I used to be so blind that I would pray "Come on in, Lord" without realizing that He was already there! We must seek the Lord that we may be enlightened and talk God's language.

His language is His Word. And, when we confess His Word back to Him in prayer, a seed is planted. That seed of faith is literally changing our situation. We cannot see it with our natural eye, but we must know and believe that God is at work. When a farmer plants a seed, he knows there will be a harvest. He doesn't see it the next day, but it is always in the "now."

> *Now faith is the substance of things hoped for, the evidence of things not seen.* ***Hebrews 11:1***

See your victory—"now." Not on tomorrow or the next day. See it now! Confess it! Believe it! Walk in it! Proclaim the victory that God has already given you and watch the Light of God shine on you.

In the Valley of . . .

Experiencing New Life

Jesus saith unto her, I that speak unto thee am he. **John 4:26**

THERE ARE SEVERAL ISSUES in this chapter that we could address. Overall, Jesus straightened out the proper way to Worship in the chapter we are reading. The woman that he would meet would know after speaking with him that there is no particular place you are required to be in order to Worship, as she had suspected. While this is very important to know, we will not focus on that within this chapter.

Before Jesus' initial conversation with this woman, He had left Judea going to Galilee. He left Judea because the Pharisees had heard that He was baptizing more candidates than John the Baptist. Jesus did not want to create a competitive scene between John the Baptist and Himself. Ultimately, He left because he wanted peace. He did not want to take any credit away from John the Baptist. Most of all, though, the scripture records that it was needful for Him to go into Samaria. Although hot, tired, thirsty and dusty, He went and His journey was long. When He arrived into the Samaritan community, He was sitting on a well. Imagine that—a well on top of a well! We quickly discover that His coming to Samaria was more than just to find a place of refreshing—He was on a mission.

The Samaritan woman that came to the well had an empty pail to draw water. According to History, it tells us that Jacob had given this well to Joseph and it had been a source of refreshment down through the centuries. Nevertheless, one thing that this well could not do was provide the entire needs that you and I have. Even though some of us may have a supply that has been provided to us from our fathers to make our lives comfortable, we must know that we need more than material provisions to quench our thirsty soul.

Jesus knew this woman's condition. He knew that her *soul* was thirsty. He knew that she had already been married five times and was presently "shacking up" with someone else. Jesus knew all of this. More importantly, He looked beyond her faults and compromising lifestyle and saw that her soul was in need. Jesus' mission at the well was to meet her need—her true need. His mission still continues. He is ready also to meet your needs. And remember, He already knows that you are thirsty!

In the midst of our hunger and thirst, there is always "stuff" that prevents us from receiving what God has ordained for us to have. In this case, there was a division between the Jews and the Samaritans. There are divisions still going on today. Yet, Jesus is always there waiting *for us* to push past the "stuff" so he can quench our thirst. Take a moment to identify the "stuff" in your life that is preventing you from reaching the Savior.

When we push past the "stuff," then God reveals to us what our weaknesses are. This woman's weaknesses were "men." According to the scripture, this woman loved men. She had a problem and apparently she thought men could satisfy it. Her problem was that she was thirsty for compassion, love, attention and, no doubt, companionship. However, there was no physical drink via any man she came in contact with that could quench her thirst everlasting—until she came in contact with the right source of water! Are you thirsty? Perhaps, you are trying to quench that thirst through your job, family, relationships or acceptance from people. Whatever you are trying to use as your "thirst quencher,"

I have come to share with you that your thirst is only satisfied when you come to Jesus. You may be dealing with lust, anger, depression or just simply, unbelief. Jesus is right here, right now to meet your need.

Everyone is important to Christ. There are no insignificant persons in the eyes of God. Your situation is not insignificant. You are important and so was the Samaritan woman. Jesus took the most talked about person whom everybody looked down upon, despised and overlooked, and He saved her. All the years that she was coming to the well, no one could help her but Jesus. He had no problem dealing with her. She was the one that had a problem dealing with Him. So it is today. Jesus does not have a problem dealing with us. Typically, we have a problem dealing with Him.

This woman began to wonder how Jesus was going to draw water from the well without a pail. She was distracted. He was there to let her know that, He was the Well.

If you do not have Jesus, you are missing out. I am not talking about being a part of a particular denomination or religion, but having Jesus in your life and daily communion with Him. "*And ye are complete in him, which is the head of all principality and power:*" **Colossians 2:10** Nothing will completely satisfy you except Jesus. This is why people are running, searching and wondering where they can go for help.

> *It is written, Man shall not live by bread alone, but by every word that proceedeth out of the mouth of God.* **Matthew 4:4b**

If you have been brought up in church, this is not good enough to save you. Even if you consider yourself to be an excellent Bible student, that is still not good enough. Only a relationship with Jesus is good enough to help your condition. Nicodemus was very smart, but Jesus told him—he must be born again. ***(John 3:3)***

> When you really get the *fullness of God,* your desires are fulfilled.

Are you thirsty? Come to the Well that does not run dry. Jesus is ready for you. He is ready right now to save you. *Do you desire a personal relationship with Jesus?*

Right now pray this prayer: "Father, I acknowledge that I have a thirst that only you can fill. I have tried many things to satisfy this thirst. But, I recognize that only you can satisfy this thirst. I am a sinner. But I believe that Jesus died for my sins and has risen again and is waiting to come into my heart. Forgive me of my sins and come into my heart. Fill me with your presence. I want new life. Thank you Lord for saving me. In Jesus Name, Amen." Now, according to ***Romans 10:9–10…*** *"That if thou shalt confess with thy mouth the Lord Jesus, and shalt believe in thine heart that God hath raised him from the dead, thou shalt be saved. For with the heart man believeth unto righteousness; and with the mouth confession is made unto salvation."*

In the Valley of . . .

A Fresh Revelation

And he spake also a parable unto them; No man putteth a piece of a new garment upon an old; if otherwise, then both the new maketh a rent, and the piece that was taken out of the new agreeth not with the old. And no man putteth new wine into old bottles; else the new wine will burst the bottles, and be spilled, and the bottles shall perish. But the new wine must be put into new bottles; and both are preserved. No man also having drunk old wine straightway desireth new: for he saith, the old is better. **Luke 5:36–38**

IN THIS VERSE, JESUS was teaching the Pharisees about a transformation and a change that could occur if they accepted it. You too, as you are reading this, can be blessed if you catch a hold of the revelation I am going to share with you. Nevertheless, you must be willing to leave any negative condition that you are in.

The revelation of this whole verse is that Jesus had come with something new. He was on the scene with a new movement. There was a new vision that was going to bring about a transformation for the whole World. He was not forcing it upon any man. Yet, He was explaining the condition for which this "new thing" could be accomplished. Jesus was trying to get the Pharisees to see that the old would not agree with the new and eventually cause conflicting results. The old what? Glad you asked. I am referring to the old traditions, opinions and methods that they were so accustomed to. Jesus was trying to get them to see that the bottle is old and different, while the wine is fresh and new. The problem is that you cannot mix something new with anything old. It just does not work. *New wine must be put into new bottles*.

What is this *new wine*? It is a new way of doing something that accomplishes the purpose of God. This new revelation is only given through Jesus Christ. However, the Pharisees did not want to accept Jesus and the liberty that He was giving. Neither do people today. They would prefer to remain traditional and stuck in their old ways.

This is what people are saying today. "I will not change because what I used to do is better. The way I used to live is better." Jesus was repeating what the people had been saying. He described the problem they would have sewing an old patch to a new garment. But even with that clear analogy, they continuously said, "I like the old." You just cannot get some people to change. Their excuse is that, "this is the environment that I was brought up in," or "this is my religion and I would prefer to keep it."

In ***Acts 15:1***, some of the brethren came down from Judea and they taught that, "You cannot be saved unless you are circumcised." People today are from all walks of life and religions and they have no new revelation or mindset of going forward. Their conversation is constantly about what used to happen. They remember how the church "used to be" and, surprisingly, they were not even there—they just heard about it!

The new wine or (revelation) that we are learning about does not destroy the foundation that we currently have, but rather builds upon it. "If the foundations be destroyed, what can the righteous do?" ***Psalms 11:3*** If you want to be blessed you must have a new revelation that builds upon the foundation that has already been laid. Wednesday will bring new experiences that Tuesday did not have.

We change by the revelation of God. The World is changing—everything is changing. We do not change the gospel, biblical principles or the doctrine that we know so well. But God reveals to us through His Son new ideas and ways of accomplishing His purpose.

> We have to be willing to accept changes that will continue to produce positive fruit in the Kingdom of God.

Some people just want to do what they have always been doing and not grow. So, again, in **Acts 15:1**, these brethren taught that you cannot be saved unless you are circumcised by the Law of Moses. Just think of how many people are hindered from receiving the gospel because of the "old wine" that people are trying to offer. When we go back to the Old Testament, Isaiah prophesied concerning new things. *"Remember ye not the former things, neither consider the things of old. Behold, I will do a new thing..."* **Isaiah 43:18** This new thing will come into reality through Christ. But unfortunately they said, "The old is better!" Are you one of them?

A lot of times, better ways are not made because we are not willing to change. We are not willing to accept new things. It is as if we are fearful that God cannot maintain us on a higher level. However, let me say to you that God is just as great on a higher level than the level that you are currently on. The scripture says, *"I will even make a way in the wilderness, and rivers in the desert."* **Isaiah 43:19b** He will bless you with what you do. *"...and be not entangled again with the yoke of bondage."* **Galatians 5:1** Forget about the old and move on to the new. *"For if I build again the things which I have destroyed, I make myself a transgressor."* **Galatians 2:18**

If you are crucified with Christ, you can live above your own opinions, ideologies and religion. Jesus brought new wine and ideas that people did not want to accept. When we learn the ways of God and get out of vast arrays of doctrine and religion, we will be blessed. *"Therefore if any man be in Christ, he is a new creature: old things are passed away: behold, all things are become new."* **II Corinthians 5:17** Circumcision has passed away. The blood of Bulls and Goats has passed away. Some of the things that you are doing have passed away. And, if you are in Christ, there is something "new" available to you. Did you notice that I said, "In Christ" not "in church?" You must be in Christ in order to receive something new. How fresh are you?

Be encouraged! Challenge yourself to leave the old for something better!

In the Valley of . . .

Regaining Your True Identity

And God said, Let us make man in our image, after our likeness: and let them have dominion over the fish of the sea, and over the fowl of the air, and over the cattle, and over all the earth, and over every creeping thing that creepeth upon the earth. So God created man in his own image, in the image of God created he him; male and female created he them. And God blessed them, and God said unto them, Be fruitful, and multiply, and replenish the earth, and subdue it: and have dominion over the fish of the sea, and over the fowl of the air, and over every living thing that moveth upon the earth.

Genesis 1:26–28

WHEN GOD CREATED MAN, He did not make him like anything else but Himself. What a Masterpiece! Man was exactly like God when he was created. God did not want man to be idle, lazy, or sitting around with nothing to do so He gave man several assignments. God's desire is to give each of us responsibility. Our responsibility is in being fruitful, multiplying, replenishing and ruling the earth. God has simply put into our hands the responsibility to manage what He has created.

This is the book of the generations of Adam. In the day that God created man, in the likeness of God made he him; Male

> *and female created he them; and blessed them, and called their name Adam, in the day when they were created. And Adam lived an hundred and thirty years, and begat a son in his own likeness, and after his image; and called his name Seth.*
>
> **Genesis 5:1–3**

Between Genesis Chapter 1 and 5, the generations that would follow after Adam were separated from God because of Adam's sin. As a result, the "*likeness*" and "*image*" of God that was once a part of Adam when he was first created was no longer there. Notice that the "*likeness*" and "*image*" that I am referring to is the spirit of man. It is through our spirit that we are eternally aware of our existence, purpose and identity. Therefore after Adam sinned, he lost his "*true*" identity. He lost the purpose of his existence and the identity that he was given from God.

God created Adam in His own image. Adam sinned and was separated from God. Adam, then, begot a son in his own likeness. When Adam's son was born, he did not have God's identity, only Adam's. Since Adam was separated from God so was his offspring. Therefore, after Adam, everyone including you was born without their "*true*" identity. Please be assured that when you look into the mirror and are pleased or displeased with what you see, this is not the identity that I am referring to. Your "*true*" identity is not your physical appearance but your spirit; that which you cannot see.

Even though man has attempted to regain his "true" character or nature, only God can restore man's "*trueness*" back to him. God had to send his Word to us to tell us who we are. ***(Refer to St. John 1:10–14)*** The Word came in the likeness of our flesh to redeem us from our lost identity. ***(Read Romans 8:3)*** If there is a "true" identity, there must be a false identity. Too many people have accepted a false identity. Pretending to be happy and content with who they think they are, they accept what is not real and authentic. Some people never address the fact that they are missing something real and genuine in their lives. What is it? It is Jesus!

> *He was in the world, and the world made by him, and the world knew him not. He came unto his own, and his own received him not. But as many as received him, to them gave he power to become the sons of God, even to them that believe on his name; Who were born, not of blood, nor of the will of the flesh, nor of the will of man, but of God. And the Word was made flesh, and dwelt among us (and we beheld his glory, the glory as of the only begotten of the Father), full of grace and truth.* **St. John 1:10–14**

There are some people who believe that we are all going to the same place once we die. This, my friend, is *not true*. If you have not been washed by the blood of Jesus Christ, not only do you have a false identity, but you also will be eternally lost if you do not repent of your sins.

We have a generation of people who are born in the likeness of Adam. And, the Bible says, "*For as in Adam all die, even so in Christ shall all be made alive.*" **I Corinthians 15:22** Before I got saved I never thought about Jesus. And, in my sins I had a false identity. "*Behold, I was shapen in iniquity; and in sin did my mother conceive me.*" **Psalms 51:5** "*The wicked are estranged from the womb: they go astray as soon as they be born, speaking lies.*" **Psalms 58:3** In other words, we are liars from birth! Why? Because we have Adam's sinful nature, not God's.

The only Person and power that can transform you and bring you into a relationship where you will be what God meant for you to be is Jesus. You cannot do this by just coming to church—you must receive Christ into your heart. "*Acquaint now thyself with him, and be at peace: thereby good shall come unto thee.*" **Job 22:21** There are so many people that are lost on today. They are really confused and do not know who they are. They have no sense of direction. Are you that individual? You do not have to be that way anymore.

"Therefore if any man be in Christ, he is a new creature: old things are passed away; behold, all things are become new." **II Corinthians 5:17** Adam failed and confused everything. Nevertheless, everything that Adam ruined, Jesus corrected. He counteracted all of Adam's confusion. So, why should we be in despair? Why should we worry? God has made it possible through Jesus Christ to bring us back to our "*true*" identity.

God is ready right now to restore you back to your "*true*" identity. Are you ready? You can take back what the enemy has stolen from you. You can have your dominion back over your home. You can take back your authority through Jesus Christ. If you have lost anything it is because the Devil has tricked and deceived you. Nevertheless, God is ready to restore. Take time now to receive your "*true*" identity.

Pray this prayer. Lord, I acknowledge that my "*true*" identity is only found in you. Come into my heart and restore me to the place that you ordained for me to be in. Make me a new creature according to Your Word! Give me new life and restore my joy, peace and hope. Thank You Jesus for saving me and giving me back my "*true*" identity.

In the Valley of . . .

Reformation versus Transformation

Behold, the days come, saith the Lord, that I will make a new covenant with the house of Israel, and with the house of Judah, Not according to the covenant that I made with their fathers in the day that I took them by the hand to bring them out of the land of Egypt, which, my covenant, they broke, although I was an husband unto them, saith the Lord; But this shall be the covenant that I will make with the house of Israel: After those days, saith the Lord, I will put my law in their inward parts, and write it in their hearts, and will be their God, and they shall be my people. And they shall teach no more every man his neighbor, and every man his brother, saying, Know the Lord; for they shall all know me, from the least of them unto the greatest of them, saith the Lord; for I will forgive their iniquity, and I will remember their sin no more.

Jeremiah 31:31–34

But now hath he obtained a more excellent ministry, by how much also he is the mediator of a better covenant, which was established upon better promises. For if that first covenant had been faultless, then should no place have been sought for the second. For finding fault with them, he saith, Behold the days come, saith the Lord, when I will make a new covenant with the house of Israel and with the house of Judah;

Hebrews 8:6–8

GOD HAS ALWAYS DEALT with mankind through a covenant. A covenant is simply an agreement between two parties to achieve a certain outcome. In this case, God's covenant with mankind was initiated by Him and only made possible by their submission to Him.

In the Old Testament, the children of Israel had a covenant with God but it was insufficient. During that time, the prophet Jeremiah recognized a nation of people who did not have a personal relationship with God. Their covenant was a national agreement. A cloud led them during the day and a pillar of fire through the night. There was no individual connection with God.

Jeremiah prophesied of a day that would come where individuals would know God for themselves and not through a corporate covenant or agreement. The covenant not only was national but it was powerless. It gave the people instructions of what they should do but it could not give them the power to carry it out. The new covenant that God would give unto Israel would draw individuals closer to Him. It would not be national but individual.

God deals with us on an individual basis. It is possible for an individual to know the Word, exercise the rituals of religion, and still not experience a relationship and true worship with God. An individual can come to church, work in the church and be a part of the church's activities and yet not have a relationship with God. This is the point where our blessings are missed.

The New and Better Covenant

If the first covenant were adequate there would not have been a need for a better one. All of us are in need of something better. We may have done something for the first time and recognized a better way to accomplish the same task. Instead of giving up, keep trying until you discover a better way.

This was the case with the Old Covenant. There had to be a better way; but there was need for blood to be shed to establish the New Covenant. The blood of bulls and goats that instituted the Old Covenant was no longer sufficient. ***(Hebrews 10:4)*** The bloodshed must come from a man! ***(Matthew 26:28)*** The man that shed the blood had to be without sin. Who else could fill this space but God's only begotten Son, Jesus? ***(Hebrews 12:24)***

Jesus laid down His life for the New Covenant. He therefore has fulfilled the requirements of God to cover the sin of mankind.

Life in the New Covenant

Reformation is different from transformation. To reform is similar to making a resolution at the beginning of the year. However, by the time February rolls around, we are back to the same habits as in previous years. To be transformed is to be given a new heart, new desires and a new purpose in life. Thus, to ask us to participate in some of our old ways is no longer of interest.

Life in the New Covenant supersedes that of the old. Our communication with God as an individual is restored through Jesus Christ. Because of our ability to communicate with God and believe by faith the promises of His Word, we are able to defeat the enemy who seeks to steal, kill and destroy.

> *Therefore if any man be in Christ, he is a new creature: old things are passed away; behold, all things are become new.*
>
> ***II Corinthians 5:17***

Notice that the scripture says, "In Christ." Not in an organization or religious group. Our life is in Christ.

Consider today whether or not you have life—life eternal. You may not have ever stepped foot into a church. Or, perhaps, you have been in church all of your life. Regardless of your background, the question still remains, "are you in Christ?"

If not, experiencing new life is very simple. As a matter of fact, it is so simple; a lot of people miss out on it. ***Romans 10:9***, says, *"That if thou shalt confess with thy mouth the Lord Jesus, and shalt believe in thine heart that God hath raised him from the dead, thou shalt be saved."*

Experiencing life in Christ is a life-changing experience. Why don't you consider Him today?

In the Valley of . . .

A Distasteful Heart

HAVE YOU EVER THOUGHT about why you need to attend Bible Study, Sunday School and Weekly Services? Have you ever stopped to consider why it is important to read your Bible on a daily basis, hiding the Word of God in your heart so that it may serve as a cornerstone for holy living? Unquestionably, it is necessary to do these things because there are so many attributes within all of our characters that do not portray the divine character of God. Did you know that? Do you agree? Right now, right where you are, there is something that God would like to change about you. This goes for all of us.

Our attendance to the Word gives the Lord the opportunity to wash away things that He does not like. We are "*growing in grace and in the knowledge of our Lord and Savior, Jesus Christ.*" ***II Peter 3:18*** Many of us have jealousy and resentment in our heart. This is distasteful unto God. He desires for us to have a pure heart. God loves us as an individual, but, He does not like what He sees in our hearts. Just as it is difficult to live in an unclean home, so it is likewise for the Lord to dwell in our hearts and our unclean temples. ***I Corinthians 3:16***

You may say, "my heart is pure." But look at the characteristics and think about yourself at this very moment. Pride; Selfishness; Disobedience; Slothfulness; Lust ... and the list continues. God does not like any of the above-referenced characteristics. In fact, He calls them abominations in His sight.

However, God gives us the opportunity to study the Word and find out exactly what it is He does not like. When you pray with a heart that is turned towards righteousness, God reveals unto you the areas that are in need of confession. The more light you allow to come into your life, darkness is exposed and will eventually disappear. You have the choice to get rid of it. Therefore, we must meditate upon God and examine ourselves against His Word.

> *These six things doth the Lord hate; yea, seven are an abomination unto him: A proud look, a lying tongue, and hands that shed innocent blood, an heart that deviseth wicked imaginations, feet that be swift in running to mischief, a false witness that speaketh lies, and he that soweth discord among brethren.*
>
> ***Proverbs 6:16***

You can never peep into a house and tell a person what is going on in there. Neither can you look through a window and explain the activities that are taking place. So unless you are in Christ, you do not know what is going on. You cannot peep in and know how the Lord operates. You must abide in Him daily. "*Abide in me, and I in you. As the branch cannot bear fruit of itself, except it abide in the vine, no more can ye, except ye abide in me.*" ***John 15:4*** Stay there and let Him work on you. Not just on Sundays, but everyday of your life. Some of us are "*ever learning and never able to come to the knowledge of the truth.*" ***II Timothy 3:7***

God is trying to prepare each of us for Heaven. But first, God wants to bless us while we are here on Earth. You do not know where you are going to be on tomorrow. That is why it is so important to take advantage of today's daily bread (Word) and apply it to your life. Otherwise, in the future, you will regret that you did not change your ways when you had the opportunity to do so. Tomorrow you may be sick. Someone you know may turn for the worse, or, death may come knocking at your door. Get your heart right while you have a chance. Today is a day of preparation.

This is no time to get involved in any unrighteousness or ungodliness. *This is a time to pray, seek God and study your Word like never before*. Find out what the Word of God says. "*The grass withereth, the flower fadeth: but the word of our God shall stand for ever.*" ***Isaiah 40:8*** The Devil comes to deceive and manipulate us into trying to find out things that have no real relevance to our walk with Christ. When we measure ourselves against God, we are nothing. The scripture says, "*The wicked shall be turned into hell, and the nations that forget God.*" ***Psalm 9:17***

It is just a matter of time before you realize that you are wrong. Do you recognize what is going on in the World today? This is no time to be slothful. ***Read Matthew 24.*** Your money is not helping you. It only helps you to buy and eat more. Can you tell me how that is helping? It doesn't help you get well or have joy. Can you see that? Therefore, you must put everything in its appropriate place and honor God.

You can waste your time, but while you are wasting time, time is running out. You only have a season. And, you better make sure that you have enough time to live right. There is nothing wrong with living prosperous and having the things that you want here on Earth. However, you have crossed the line when what you have replaces your commitment to God. The Lord hates this and the only thing that can help you is the Word of God. *The Word of God has to wash away our sins*.

We spend our time talking about things that we really do not know about and the Lord is not pleased. Some people will drive a mile to talk about somebody and won't go a block to be a part of Sunday School. The Lord hates this. People will spend $10 to take you out to lunch to run down the church; yet, they will complain when asked to put $3 into the offering. Do not be the person with a distasteful heart which the Lord hates. No matter where you go in this World, somebody sees what you are doing. Live right and it will pay off after awhile.

Something that is distasteful is not worth keeping. The dictionary describes it as "*not pleasing*." Can you think of a time when you tasted something that was gross? The first thing that probably came to mind was to spit it out. The condition of our heart can be nauseating to the Lord. One minute we are one way, the next minute another. We are lukewarm! The Word says, "*So then because thou are lukewarm, and neither cold nor hot, I will spue thee out of my mouth.*" ***Revelation 3:16***

The choice is yours. You have the opportunity to get your heart right before God. Find out in His Word what pleases Him. When you obey His Word, you will not be disappointed!

Section Two

His Poverty, My Riches

In the Valley of . . .

Agreeing with God

WHATSOEVER YOU RELEASE here on earth will be released in heaven ***(Matthew 18:18).*** It starts with *you*. Did *you* know that? If you want something to be released into your hands, don't wait on heaven. *Heaven is waiting on you!* You have to let it go. The way you let it go is by releasing it. How do you release it? *By Faith*. There is not one problem that you may have which will benefit you. So, you have to ignore your problems and act as if they do not even exist.

I had an experience where my head was hurting extremely bad. I had to quote a scripture to this headache that kept coming back. That scripture was ***Amos 3:3***; "*Can two walk together, except they be agreed?*" So, I told the headache that I didn't agree with it; therefore, it can no longer walk with me. The headache wanted me to agree with it, but I did not. Neither should you. You do not have to agree with the pains that are in your body. If those pains do not agree with you, then you must release them!

You have to learn to talk silly. You are not talking to yourself, but to a spirit that is trying to overtake you. And not only are you talking to that spirit, but to several spirits. For instance, if you give in to the spirit of *poverty* then the next spirit that you will give in to is *oppression*. The Devil is not satisfied with just attacking you one way. He wants to bring you down with as many spirits as he possibly can. If you accept what he brings your way, this means that you agree with it. You never agree with anything that is trying to kill you or bring you down.

There are some people who say, "I feel like I am catching a cold." When you say this, whether you realize it or not, you are agreeing with something that is against you having a healthy body.

> We use words that condemn us without fully recognizing what we are saying.

You are not going to live on this earth without having a struggle against the powers of darkness, the prince of the power of the air, and principalities ***(Ephesians 2:2, 6:12).*** Everything that you have comes from somewhere. There is a spiritual world up there that attacks the physical world down here. So we must know how to deal with the Enemy of our soul and spirit. Just saying, "Hallelujah," is not enough. Coming to church and singing in the choir, is not nearly enough. It is your knowledge about God and your ability to apply it that gives you the victory.

In which in times past ye walked according to the course of this world, according to the prince of the power of the air, the spirit that now worketh in the children of disobedience.

Ephesians 2:2

For we wrestle not against flesh and blood, but against principalities, against powers, against the rulers of the darkness of this world, against spiritual wickedness in high places.

Ephesians 6:12

You have to let the Devil know that you know Jesus. You must let him know that Jesus died for your sins and that you have redemption through His name. You have to talk to the Devil just like you talk to anyone else. You must tell him what you **do not** want. The Devil is like a salesman. He will try to sell you a lot of things that are no good for you. A lot of things would not be upon us if we just did not accept them. The Devil will ring our doorbell (our minds and consciences) and make us offers constantly. You do not have to answer the door. Ignore his offers!

Why would we agree with things that disagree with us? Why would we agree with sickness and poverty and the things of the Devil? These are offers which must be ignored. Think about it. You are walking with something that is killing you. You *do not* have to… it is your choice. One reason why this occurs is because for some strange reason people like to agree with un-agreeable circumstances. It seems to soothe their appetite and meet their needs.

The Bible is like a cookbook, containing a variety of menus. What you must know how to do is place your order, the Chef is on duty 24 hours a day, 7 days a week. In our spiritual cookbook, Jesus, the Chef, tells you in the Word that He is the Bread of Life! Further, not only is He the Bread if Life, if you are thirsty, you can come to Him and drink. Do you agree with that? You should!

When we start doing what God wants us to do, we quickly see how things start working in our favor. Sometimes, though, what he wants us to do is unpleasant. As a matter of fact, most of the time when He asks us to do something, we have to fight within ourselves before we "*agree*" to do it. There were things that God told me to do that I really did not want to do. Yet, I did them and was blessed by my obedience. God does not give us everything in detail. We want Him to spell it out and lay out the entire plan before we make one move. He does not work this way.

In ***Galatians 3:6***, the scripture records that Abraham believed God and it was accounted to him for righteousness. Yet, in ***Hebrews 11:17***, the scripture records that he acted on what he believed. *There are many people who believe but never act on what they believe.* There is a difference between belief and faith. To believe only is not enough. To have faith is to believe and act on what you believe. God responds to our faith. *"But without faith it is impossible to please Him: for He that cometh to God must believe that He is, and that He is a rewarder of them that diligently seek Him."* ***Hebrews 11:6*** This is where we make so many mistakes. We talk about what we believe, but never turn it into faith and do anything about it.

A lot of people believe in paying tithes, witnessing and praying. However, when it comes to placing those beliefs into action, faith becomes apparently absent. What good is it then to *just believe?*

God has a blessing for you and you can have the victory if you agree with Him! The Pharisees did not agree with God. The Jews did not agree with God. Pharaoh did not agree with God. Nevertheless, the Hebrew Boys agreed with God and because they did, He brought them out. Joseph agreed with God and because he did, God delivered him. When we come to the New Testament, the woman with the issue of blood agreed with God, and was made whole. If you agree with God, you can be healed and experience a life full of victories.

Well, what if you are sick and you say that you are healed. Is that lying? No. The Bible says that you were healed and if you were healed, you are healed. ***(I Peter 2:24)*** *"Death and life are in the power of the tongue: and they that love it shall eat the fruit thereof."* ***Proverbs 18:21*** Just because you feel one way does not mean you are that way. *You do not have to die just because you feel like dying.* We do not live by our feelings. We have to be careful of not letting doubt creep into our lives. Some things that appear so innocent and harmless can be the most deadly. Remember, just like "life" is in the tongue so is "death." If you are going to follow Jesus, then follow Him. Agree with His Word. *"Abstain from all appearance of evil."* ***I Thessalonians 5:22*** You do not lose anything when you agree with God. Nothing at all. Be strong in the Lord! He is faithful that promised. Do you agree?

In the Valley of . . .

Claiming God's Promises

THERE IS SOMETHING MORE to each of us than others see. Would you agree? We typically judge each other by the outward appearance. We have talents, abilities and potentials that others cannot see. But, God knows all things. You would be surprised to know the potentials buried in the individuals living in your household. Furthermore, you would be surprised to learn of the success hidden within yourself. If we would let God work within us and work out of us the potentials that are already there, we would be doing a lot more than what we are presently occupied with. Sadly, we sit down on the gifts that he has given us while we continue to ask His blessings upon us. God has put within us power and dominion to bless others and ourselves. What else do we want God to do? Why do we need to pray for God to push us? This is not necessary.

The dominion that was given to Adam and Eve is yet a part of you. It was given back to us through Jesus Christ. When you receive God in your life, you receive everything that you need to accomplish His purpose. Everything that God has for you is for you. It is for you naturally and spiritually. God has something within you that you have not believed Him for. Do you accept that? Sometimes it is because of fear, slothfulness, and/or just a lack of knowledge.

We cannot operate for God in the natural. So, then, we must pray and seek for God in the supernatural. When we do this, we always have the victory.

> *Giving thanks unto the Father, which hath made us meet to be partakers of the inheritance of the saints in light: Who hath delivered us from the power of darkness, and hath translated us into the kingdom of his dear Son: In whom we have redemption through his blood, even the forgiveness of sins.*
>
> **Colossians 1:12–14**

This scripture is very important to us. Please notice the word, "hath." This word indicates that there is something that has already taken place. It is something that is phrased in the past tense.

In the first two verses, the word, "*hath*" is particularly noted. In the third verse, the word, "*have*" is noted. So, what I am saying to you is that we have (presently) because he hath (prior to now) already done what is required for us to have the victory. If you do not have what you want from God, it is not because he has not provided it. It is because of a lack of knowledge. The words "*In whom*" relates to the Person, Jesus. This is a formula for anything that you want from God. God has provided everything. This is the joy that we have in the Word of God. It is the very fact that He has already done it. Done what? Everything necessary for us to live victoriously, enjoy life and live eternally with Him!

What you want from God, you already "*have*" *right now!* Do you realize that? It has already been provided. I cannot stress this enough. If we do not take the Word of God for what it is telling us, than we are limiting ourselves to what we feel is obtainable in the natural sense. But, the very thing that you do not see is available to you—now. If you do not have it now, you will never have it. How is that? Because it is only what you receive "now" in your spirit by faith that materializes in the natural. If you cannot receive by faith "now," it is impossible for you to experience its manifestation. "*Now* faith is the substance of things hoped for... That word, "*now*" is so very important. It means just what is says—now—at this very moment!

> *Who his own self bare our sins in his own body on the tree, that we, being dead to sins, should live unto righteousness: by whose stripes ye were healed.* **I Peter 2:24**

Peter was an actual eyewitness to the life of Jesus. And he is writing because he had firsthand experience. Therefore, He could write that *he bare our sins*. This is a statement of fact. It was Jesus Who died for you. This is a reality. And, through His death, you have life—now. In order for us to receive what God has given we must agree with His Word. We must speak it as it is written in the Word. There is nothing left for us to do but believe.

My wife and I went to South Carolina and there was a lady who had left her luggage at the airport. While we were there we took her to the airport. What we discovered, though, was that she had to "claim" her luggage! The luggage was hers. It had been at the airport for about a week. Nevertheless, she had to present her "claim ticket" to get what was hers. She had to claim it even though it was already hers. It was bought and paid for. But in order for her to get it, she had to claim it. Do you think you can just sit where you are and think that you are going to get something from God? Not so. You must claim what God has given you. You will not get it unless you first believe that it is yours. Secondly, you will not receive it unless you claim it. You have to open up your mouth and began to confess what the Word of God says. Forget what your friends have said. Ignore what your teacher told you. Do away with your parents said. What has God said about you? Do you know?

What is the "claim slip?" It is your faith. It is your obedience. When you present this claim slip unto God, it will not be ignored or denied.

You have to always live in the "now!" Act like you have something—now.

Let me share something with you that is very powerful. Jesus said that He is the Way, the Truth and the Life! ***(St. John 14:6)*** You don't ever have to wait for God to make a way for you. He is the Way and the way is always provided. If you are waiting for another way to appear, then maybe you should continue waiting. If you are waiting for your job to make a way, keep waiting. If you are waiting for the government to make something happen, perhaps you have a while to wait. If you are waiting for your community to make a way, just keep waiting. But Jesus is the Way! This is present tense. Right now—He is the Way. He is the way through your circumstances. Get into the "now" and see how powerful He is to change your life.

God hath qualified us to receive His blessings. How has he qualified us? It is done through the blood of Jesus. God must see the blood of Jesus over us. When we are covered under Jesus' blood, we are made partakers! We can have anything we want or say according to His will ***(I John 5:14–15)***.

Galatians 3:13 states that, "*He hath redeemed us from the curse of the law*" found in ***Deuteronomy 28:15–30***. Don't live like you are under a curse. If you are saved, act like it! You are redeemed from the curse of the law. The curse of the law includes *poverty, sickness and spiritual death*. If you are redeemed from this curse then you can claim your *prosperity, physical health, and, of course, eternal life!* You don't have to go to a Witch Doctor or a Fortune Teller. Jesus is within you and His power is available to you.

Finally, allow me to share this powerful principle with you. Let God be the Object of your faith. If God is the Object of your faith, you will always see faith work for you. However, if you put your faith into people, places and things, your faith will fail. Why? People, places and things are unreliable. While it may seem stable today, who knows about tomorrow? Yet, you can ALWAYS rely on God! He is the same yesterday, today and forever. ***(Hebrews 13:8)*** God moves our mountains when we have faith in Him. If we have faith that our own strength will move the mountain, we will continuously lose out in this spiritual walk. If your ability could move mountains, you would not be in the condition that you are in today. However, if you face reality, the mountains in your life are still there because you are incapable of moving them on your own. But God can move those mountains for you if you just have faith in Him. Let the problem that you have be cast into the sea and watch it drown!

Claim God's Promises and watch them come to pass in your life!

In the Valley of . . .

Receiving the Blessing of Abraham

"NOW WE BRETHREN, AS Isaac was, are the children of promise" ***Galatians 4:28***. What does it mean to be as Isaac? What was Isaac? According to ***Romans 4:3***, *"For what saith the scripture? Abraham believed God and it was counted unto him for righteousness."* ***Galatians 3:6*** says again that *"Abraham believed God and it was credited unto him for righteousness."* Isaac was the son of Abraham, and he who believes is the same as Abraham's children. It is important to understand our positions in Christ so that we can understand what has been promised to us. There are so many believers living beneath their privileges simply because they don't realize what is available to them. They don't know how to receive because they do not understand God. ***John 8:32*** says, "You shall know the truth and the truth shall set you free." Only the truth that you know will make us free, but we must understand how to apply that truth. Then we must have faith to live by that truth. That's why the Bible, over and over again, teaches and emphasizes that we walk by faith. ***Romans 1:17*** says, "For therein is the righteousness of God revealed from faith to faith: as it is written, the just shall live by faith." ***Galatians 3:11*** and ***Hebrews 10:38*** speaks regarding the just walking by faith. We need to understand the principles of faith and how to apply them under all circumstances.

We need to know how to find the principles in our Bibles without opening our Bibles. Realize that Christianity is not a *religious* thing; rather, it is a *holy* thing. We need to be able to recall God's promises at any time, under any circumstance. The beginning of God's promises to us, are instituted in ***Genesis 12***. All of it had its commencement in Abraham. First, God told Abraham to leave his relatives and that which was familiar and comfortable, without great detail or specific direction. God just told him to leave and go to a certain place. Abraham responded in two ways: To begin, he just *believed* God. Secondly, he *obeyed* God. Believing God is meaningless without obedience to Him. So, without question or complaint, Abraham left with nothing except instruction.

When Abraham was about 75, God made a promise to Abraham, and Abraham had to wait 24 years before the promise was fulfilled. God told him that He would give him a seed. That seed would be named Isaac. From Isaac, a nation extending through the generations of time would be born. This nation was the Jews.

God fulfilled his promise after years of Abraham facing oppositions. Before God fulfills His promises to us, we will go through hardships. We can do ourselves a favor by standing still and seeing the salvation of the Lord in the midst of our circumstances. Stand still and see God working on our behalves, because we have to prove ourselves in our current circumstances before God will help us go further. We want God to bless us and God wants to bless us. He sent Jesus to die in order that we may experience blessings. God has blessings laid up in heaven for people who have never taken the extra step to receive them. Look at this: There are three reasons why they have never received their blessings. First of all, they did not know they were there for them. Second of all, some people did not believe that they had blessings waiting on them, and thirdly, they failed to obey. Simply, we must be willing and obedient.

Abraham was not the best person in the world, so stop beating yourself up over past mistakes or even those in the present. There is nobody in the Bible who was perfect except Jesus. All of them made mistakes, all of them did something wrong. For example, Moses committed murder; Samson laid the source of strength in the deceitful lap of Delilah; and David committed adultery. Yet, God, in His infinite mercy, saw how he could use them anyway to accomplish purpose for the Kingdom.

As God reveals himself to us and extends knowledge and understanding of how to walk in the light of revelation, God will bless us. However, this is a two-way street: God cannot reveal anything fresh and anew unto us until we have obeyed that which he has already revealed to us. Obeying God should be the first thing on our agendas. The Bible says in ***Deuteronomy 29:29***, *"The secret things belong unto God, but the things that are revealed belong to the children of God, you and your children."* God reveals enough to us for us to obey him and for us to be blessed.

It is amazing how, after man sinned, God had a plan that would give all people of this world a chance to be saved. He said all nations will be blessed in Abraham, long after Abraham was gone. That blessing is Jesus. He delivered us from the curse of the law. According to ***Galatians 3:13***, *"Christ redeemed us from the curse of the law by becoming a curse for us, for it is written: 'Cursed is everyone who is hung on a tree.'* " No flesh can be justified by the law because by the law is knowledge of sin. The law will tell us what to do, but it does not have the power to make us do it. *"For while the law was weak in the flesh,"* according to ***Romans 8***, *"God sent His own son in the likeness of flesh to condemn sin in the flesh."* Now we have everything at our disposal that God had promised through Abraham.

Jesus made all the promises that God made to Abraham possible. He delivered us from the curse of the law by being made a curse for us. The curse of the law was three-fold: poverty, sickness, and spiritual death. We are all Gentiles. And if you belong to Christ, then you are Abraham's seed according to ***Galatians 3:29***, and heirs according to this promise. The key to unlocking this promise, however, is belonging to Christ. God kept Abraham in the forefront because Abraham obeyed God. It is found throughout the Bible that the just shall live by faith. (See ***Romans 1:17, 3:11***, and ***Hebrews 10:38***). ***II Corinthians 5:7*** says that, "*we shall walk by faith—not by sight*"; not by knowledge, not by expertise. ***Hebrews 11:1*** says that "*faith is the substance of things hoped for and the evidence of things not seen.*" Hope has no tangible substance. There's nothing in hope. You can say, "I hope I get a job," but with hope alone, you will never get one. You can say, "I hope God will heal me"; He will never heal you. It is impossible to please God without faith. You *must* have faith. He who comes to God must first believe, and we are always coming to God for something.

Whatever the circumstances are, we must believe that God is a rewarder of those who diligently seek Him. We don't please God because we come to church. We don't please God because we dress up. We don't please God because we preach. We don't please God because we do good deeds for other people. Deeds don't mean a thing without faith. We're justified only by faith. The Bible says in ***Romans 5:1***, "*Therefore being justified by faith we have peace with God through Jesus Christ.*" **Acts 13:39** says that we are "*justified from all things when we could not be justified from the Law of Moses.*" The law could not justify us. The law was not able; it was weak.

Just as Isaac was, so we are also the children of the covenant promise. The Bible tells us that we have the same privileges; we have the same relationship that Abraham had with God. Abraham obeyed God and it was accounted unto him for righteousness. God was pleased with Abraham, although Abraham did not have what Jesus had. Jesus is the only one who could fully please God. He met all of God's requirements. We come to God and we just want to feel good. However, we would not have a good time if our faith was not increased. If we receive faith and can apply that faith to every circumstance that we meet, then we can say that we had a good time. Not only did we have a good time, but we have victory. We need victory to hold our peace. We need victory to overcome things within us. We need to know that no matter what happens, we yet have a refuge. We need to know that when trouble comes, we have a defense. We need to know how to make the statement of faith that the Lord lives and is on our side, even in the midst of adversity. Jesus said, *"Whatsoever you ask in prayer, believing, ye shall receive,"* ***Matthew 21:22***. If we don't have faith when we ask, how can we receive?

Obedience is better than sacrifice. We make all kinds of commendable sacrifices, but obedience to God is far greater. It is obedience to God that will bring the results of our sacrifices. There was a time when God used Paul to anoint people with blessed handkerchiefs. We don't have to use that method unless God tells us to, because God had a purpose for doing what He did, the way He did it. God gave us faith and He gives us power through the Holy Ghost. There is nothing like the power of the Holy Ghost! When we use our own power, we can't love our enemies. We can't be faithful. We can't look too far beyond ourselves and the limits we possess. We can't even make a good sacrifice for a ministry. But when we have the Holy Ghost power, we can do it. We can be effective witnesses.

God does a lot of things that do not make sense. Isaac was a type of Christ because he was a promised son. Jesus was a promised son and He fulfilled all the promises God made through Abraham. It took the supernatural power of God for Sarah, who at the age of almost 100 with Abraham to bring forth a son. It took the supernatural power of God for Mary, without a relationship with a man, to also bring forth a son. In ***Genesis 22***, God told Abraham to *"take his own son and offer him up as a sacrifice."* Jesus was offered up for our sins. Isaac was a forerunner, in some sense of the sacrifice that Jesus would eventually make for our sins. Abraham took Isaac up on the mountain, while Isaac wondered where the sacrificial offering was. Abraham asked him not to worry because his faith knew that the Lord would make proper provision. Upon placing Isaac as the sacrifice, Abraham, yet obeying God, drew his sword back, and according ***Hebrews 11***, *"he believed that even if he killed Isaac, God would raise him up."* What an awesome demonstration of complete faith! How far would you have gone? In the same manner, Jesus laid down his life, and advised that on the third day, God would raise him up. And on the third day, Jesus was out of the grave, holding the keys to death and hell, with ALL power in His hands. To begin, nobody really believed it would happen, but trust that whatever God says, it is sure to come to pass.

God tells us to do certain things, and we fret because we do not see the outcome right away. The first thing we think about is how the situation is going to totally affect us. For instance, we say, "If I give my last $10, how am I going to get gas tonight after I leave church"? or "How am I going to feed my kids"? or "How will this shorten my ability to pay my rent"? As opposed to faith, these are the first things we not only think about, but speak about, not realizing that the last penny we give, could result in God paying for everything, without attachment because we were obedient. The reason Abraham was blessed was because God told Abraham to leave. God did not go into detail saying, "Now when you get five miles down the road there's a well of water; you won't have to thirst. When you get five miles down the road again, a truck will come along and you won't have to keep walking." God never even gave him a map! He just simply told Abraham to "Go." Our problem with obedience stems from wanting God to spell out everything. *Newsflash*, my friends—That's not faith!

We need to let God know our needs. He already knows, but God wants us to talk to Him. We don't send God a note across the church. We don't send God a fax. It says confess with your mouth; believe in your heart. He's there. The reason that sometimes we are not blessed is because we don't talk to God. We don't express what's going on within us to God. We have a high priest who cannot be touched with the feelings of our infirmities. God already knows our thoughts; he knows our tomorrows. God wants us to talk because He wants us to know that He is there.

Once we develop constant relationships with God, He will give us boldness to do things because God wants us to be blessed people. We have to tell people when we see things in their lives that are wrong. We are afraid to say things like that because people might leave church. So what? If they leave saved, what difference does it make? God gets the glory. If they stay in the church as hypocrites, God does not get the glory. Don't be afraid of people; treat people right. That's why the prophets got in trouble—they were afraid of people. Read the Old Testament.

We ought to be hungry and thirsty for righteousness and seek God until he comes and reigns in righteousness. In Egypt, the people didn't have anything and in the wilderness they did not have enough. But when they got to Canaan they had more than enough because God is more than enough. God is able. Now what is it that God can't do that you need done? Is it healing? God can do it. You might have to spend a night in prayer. It's time to seek the Lord until He comes and rains righteousness that is visible manifested in your life.

Righteousness is not what we do for God; it's what God does for us. I know what it means to pray long hours; I know what is means to lay before the Lord. And I know what it means for folks to talk about you, while you are saying, "God forgive them." We have the victory when we say, "Lord, forgive them." While Stephen was being stoned, he looked up and saw Jesus standing by the right hand of God, and he said forgive them. **(Acts 7:54–60)** Then, after this tragic event, God saved Saul/Paul. He had courage because he said, *"Things that were gain to me, I count them as loss that I might win more of Christ."* In other words, Paul looked at his life, analyzed it and found that with all he had accomplished, he was willing to count it as loss to gain Christ alone. For he who seeks to save his life shall lose it; but he who loses his life for the sake of Christ shall save it. We are going to have to lay down something. When people play cards, they have to lay down some cards. We have to lay down some cards. They may not all be aces, they may not all be queens, but we're going to lay down something.

We are the children of promise. God's promise to Abraham was fulfilled through Jesus Christ. We all have an opportunity to eat at the same table. Jesus has other sheep that are not of this fold who have been called under this umbrella of salvation and He stands as the Chief Shepherd. Through the faith of Abraham, God used him to reach thousands. There are many people, who make promises and break them, but God does not return any of His promises void—they are all fulfilled. He has never has broken a promise. If we obey Him, we will receive all of His promises as they pertain to our divine call and purpose.

Section Three

Spiritual Development

In the Valley of . . .
"On The Job" Training

And not only so, but we glory in tribulations also: knowing that tribulation worketh patience; and patience, experience; and experience, hope: **Romans 5:3–4**

Tribulation

HAVE YOU EVER ASKED God for patience? You may not have known, but according to the scripture, before there is patience there is tribulation. Do not ask for patience if you do not want tribulation. Some people pray, "Lord, I want patience, and give me patience *right now!*" Suddenly, we experience a series of tribulations and then immediately say, "Deliver me Lord, *right now!*" This chapter will help you realize that God is trying to give you patience through tribulations to increase your knowledge of Him.

Interestingly, the right perspective of dealing with tribulations is to glory in them. If you want God to bless you, you must learn to do this. What are tribulations? They are difficult circumstances, hard times, and unpleasant experiences that we go through at various times in our life. Normally, we do not like to hear the word 'tribulation.' But in the midst of our tribulation, we learn patience. Some people think that they can just be patient. This is not possible. At times, it is difficult to bring ourselves, yes this body of flesh, under spiritual subjection. Therefore, tribulation works on us and after awhile we recognize that we are developing patience.

Have you ever been in a Doctor's Office and watched various people in the waiting room? They are constantly picking up reading material, glancing at the television, going outside to walk around and take a smoke and then coming back in to wait some more. When you are really patient, you sit still with confidence. Tribulation works patience within you. When you are trusting in God, you cannot do anything but wait on the Lord. And while you are waiting on the Lord, He is teaching you. If you are all upset and restless on the inside, you might as well admit that you do not have patience. So tribulations come to make us be still, calm and confident in the Lord.

Patience

Patience is one of those characteristics that most of us do not have. We need patience, though. We are routinely in a hurry because everything around us is push-button, instantaneous and automatic. Just look around. You have fast-food, automated teller machines, microwaves, remotes, self-check out counters and the list goes on. Most of us no longer have house phones because cellular phones are the mode by which we use to communicate as we are "on the go." As a society, things are made for the person who is in a hurry. We can even drink our lunch out of a can to lose weight, just in case we do not find time to physically go into a work out facility. Are all of these amenities really good for us? I do not believe so, simply because it stifles patience and causes us to treat God in like manner. "*In your patience possess ye your soul.*" **Luke 21:19** "*For ye have need of patience, after that ye have done the will of God, ye might receive the promise.*" **Hebrews 10:36** Sometimes we pray for God to deliver us from some things, when instead we should find ourselves waiting on God because His objective is teaching us patience. Hold on and wait on the Lord. "*Men ought always to pray, and not to faint:*" **Luke 18:1**

Experience

Patience brings you to experience. Experience is something that you have already come through. It is something that you have done which has molded your character. Do you want to have experience? Unfortunately, experience does not come by reading books—Not even this one! Experience comes by *"On the Job" Training*. You do not go to college and get experience. You learn how to deal with things. You learn how to put everything in its perspective place. If you want some experience, you must get involved. Whatever your hands find to do, you should do it with all of your might. Experience does not come without error, so that is why it is important to first develop a level of patience.

David was able to conquer Goliath because of his experience with the bear. We do not want to deal with the bear, but we want to face Goliath. You need to face the bear first and bring that first-place ribbon of victory home. After that victory, you are able to deal with things because you have something under your belt named experience. God will not put any more on you than you can withstand. However, you must be willing to learn a little at a time and get stronger and stronger day by day. To do this, you must learn the Word and walk by faith. You need faith. But you also need *"On the Job" Training*. When you have the opportunity to do any thing for God, you should do it. No matter how small a job it may appear to be.

God will never send you to a higher level until you have learned something by experience on the lower level. We try to mount up like the Eagle, according to the Scripture in **Isaiah 40:31**. But, really, we do not understand how the Eagle mounts up. The Eagle soars with the wind. He flies high because of the wind. We try to fly high in our own strength. We fail to soar with the Spirit which represents the wind in the scripture. Therefore, we get tired and give up easily. Never forget that the works of the flesh will tire you out. But when you know the Lord is within you, nothing or no one else disturbs you. Nothing anyone else says discourages you.

> *But they that wait upon the Lord shall renew their strength; they shall mount up with wings like eagles; they shall run, and not be weary; and they shall walk, and not faint.* **Isaiah 40:31**

Many times the Devil defeats us because we fail to conquer anything in our life. We are always complaining and giving up. You may not understand why you are going through something. But the Lord is right there with you and He is your help. But, it is up to you to hold on and be strong. I must encourage you to, "*look unto Jesus, Who is the author and finisher of your faith.*" **Hebrews 12:2** Also, you must, "*Set your affections on things above, not on things on the earth.*" **Colossians 3:2** You will miss the mark if you follow everything down here on Earth.

You are the seed that God has planted in the soil. And, eventually, somewhere in your life you are going to germinate and bring forth fruit. David said, "*I waited patiently for the Lord; and He inclined unto me, and heard my cry.*" **Psalms 40:1** If you do not become patient in this walk of faith, you will never bring forth any fruit. Do you want to be blessed? You cannot just walk in a church and receive all that God has for you in one setting. You, at some point, must have tribulations, patience, experience and hope.

Always remember when you come through all of this, you will have more blessings, wisdom and understanding. Then, you will know how to relate to God even the more. This is His desire—"*That [we] may know Him, and the power of His resurrection, and the fellowship of His sufferings.*" **Philippians 3:10**

In the Valley of . . .

Human Insufficiencies

Not that we are sufficient of ourselves to think any thing as of ourselves; but our sufficiency is of God; **II Corinthians 3:5**

HUMAN INSUFFICIENCY IS ONE of our major problems. There are many things that we would like to do, but are unable to because of our insufficiencies. *This is why we need Jesus*. Every one has certain limitations. If you haven't reached them yet, you eventually will.

Your abilities can only take you so far before you recognize how frail and weak you really are. But, if God is working in your life, by faith, you can overcome all of these obstacles. In other words, your inabilities are opportunities for God to show Himself strong in your life.

When you observe the things going on in the world, it depicts an image of people stepping into quicksand. When you step into quicksand, you cannot save yourself. You need someone to pull you out. And, the harder you try to get out on your own, the quicker you go down. Quicksand is very deceiving. But, thank God for Jesus—He came to pull us out! All you have to do is ask Him to save you. "*And it shall come to pass that whosoever shall call on the name of the Lord shall be saved.*" **(Acts 2:21)**

Just like the analogy of quicksand, likewise, you cannot overcome the things of the world without Him in your life. You may take another college course, get a promotion on your job or move into a new community. Yet, you are still in the same predicament.

> You are the same everywhere you go *unless the Lord Jesus changes your heart.*

If He is living within you, then you have overcome the world. How? Because He has overcome the world! ***(I John 5:4, 5)*** Just because you may go to church and sing or preach does not mean that you have overcome the world. You must be born again. ***(St. John 3:5–7)*** We have overcome the world by the blood of the Lamb and the word of our testimonies, not by church membership or affiliation. ***(Revelations 12:11)***

> *For whatsoever is born of God overcometh the world; and this is the victory that overcometh the world, even our faith. Who is he that overcometh the world, but he that believeth that Jesus is the Son of God?* **I John 5:4, 5**

There are many people who are struggling when they do not have to. They are fighting when they are not required to. The only fight that the Saints should participate in is the "*good fight of faith.*" ***(I Timothy 6:12)***

There is nothing hard for God ***(Jeremiah 32:17)***. However, there are a lot of things that are too hard for us to do without Him. David was up against a nine foot giant named Goliath. Some of us are up against nine feet circumstances named ill heath, financial difficulty, bankruptcy, repossessions, addictions, foreclosures and many more that would never end this list. These are things that are too big for us to bring down on our own. Can you think of something in your life that is too big for you to handle? If so, put it into God's hands. Paul said, "*I can do all things through Christ which strengthens me*" ***Philippians* 4:13**. "*Cast your cares upon him for he careth for you.*" **I Peter 5:7**

The nature of a baby is to lay its head upon its mother's shoulder. Regardless of what is going on with the mother, the baby is resting on her shoulder. God wants us to rest in Him the same way. It is so difficult for us to get to the place where we can "*rest in the Lord.*" ***Psalms 37:7*** We do all we can to perfect our insufficiencies without God's help. This prevents us from resting in the Lord. There are some human insufficiencies that He allows to remain; yet His grace is sufficient to sustain us in this life. ***(Read the following scriptures—Psalms 138:8, Philippians 1:6, II Corinthians 12:9)***

Peter thought that he was a good fisherman. However, one night he toiled and toiled and caught no fish. He had just discovered his insufficiency. You know, sometimes you can be working, living and going along as if you are sufficient within yourselves. It may seem like you are doing okay with your formal training, years of experience and relationships with others. Eventually you will experience a roadblock where you need help and can go no further. So Jesus came along and told Peter to let his net down. When Peter obeyed, they caught more fish than their net could handle. ***(Luke 5:4)*** Things seem to go well within our own expertise. They go extremely better, however, when we surrender both our abilities and inabilities to Jesus. Just ask Peter!

When God calls us to His work, He equips us for the job. A lot of times we hesitate to move forward by faith because of our insufficiencies. But God knows what is best. Countless times, He has used individuals to accomplish His will. Remember Moses? He wanted Aaron to speak for Him. It angered the Lord and He had to show Moses what He could do through Him in spite of His insufficiencies. ***(Read Exodus 6th Chapter)*** What about Abel, Enoch, Noah and Abraham? These are all individuals who were mightily used of God to accomplish His Will, all with human insufficiencies and imperfect in various ways. ***(Read Hebrews 11:4–11)***

My brothers and sisters, "*...seeing we also are compassed about with so great a cloud of witnesses, let us lay aside every weight...*" ***Hebrews 12:1*** Lay aside the weight of doubt. Lay aside the weight of hesitation. Accept the call of God in spite your insufficiencies and watch Him perform a miracle in your life!

Jesus uses our insufficiencies for His Glory!

In the Valley of . . .

Sowing In Difficult Times

Then Isaac sowed in that land, and received in the same year a hundredfold: and the Lord blessed him. **Genesis 26:12**

Looks Can Be Deceiving

WHEN THINGS START GOING wrong, if we fail to believe God, we will look for something elsewhere. We normally search for something that *looks better* than where we are. You cannot listen to your imagination. Your imagination can take you places that your body cannot go. It seems like nothing is happening where we are. But, wherever you are, if God is there, something is happening. You cannot make things happen on your own. But when you and I believe God, you better believe something is happening.

If we look around there will always be unpleasant things. It may be family problems, job problems, and even personal problems. There was a problem when Isaac sowed—a great problem. There was a famine in the land. Everyone was leaving to go down into Egypt. But God told Isaac to stand still. Egypt symbolized the world. Canaan was the Promised Land. Never leave something good to go to something bad. The world can entice you, making you believe that what is bad is actually good. *Be careful!* Because, for the most part, what we may believe to be good, really turns out to be bad.

Are you wandering from place to place? Or, maybe, you are just wondering if another place would be better than where you are. Let me encourage you to *stand still.*

> The space between the promise and the blessing is the time of yielding to the divine will of God.

Before God blesses any of us, we will have to do a whole lot of things that we do not want to do. Because the ways and plans of God are non-humanistic and unattainable, we will not be blessed until we do certain things that go against natural feelings. For instance, we will find ourselves embracing the person that we do not like, opening our hearts to change, or even forgiving someone for past hurts because it is God's way. Like it or not, God is not going to bless us until we become a doer of His precious Word. God is saying, "I am not doing anything until you obey." God did not bless Isaac until he obeyed His command and stayed. You and I must also obey God before we are blessed. If we do not do what the Word says, consequently, we will not be blessed. We must pray and be faithful. God has an agenda and a principle that we must abide by and that becomes our roadmap for reaching our destiny in Christ.

It is not unusual for most of us to wait for the right time to do what God requires of us. However, God requires us to sow in difficult times. He wants to see if we can stand the pressure. It is in those times when some of us think that we are going to die when we go through certain things. There are some people who commit suicide because they cannot take the pain. But God knows how to take us through things where we do not feel the pain. Do you remember Job? In the nine months of his suffering, Job struggled, yet survived. He vowed not to curse God and in the end, reaped a harvest double the seeds he had planted!

Receiving the Blessing

Do you think that God does not want to bless you? He desires to bless you. However, when He begins to bless you, somebody will envy you. Some of your friends will stop associating with you. Somebody will lie on you. But, do not cry...Praise the Lord! No person can stop God from fulfilling His promise. The more you go through and suffer, the greater your blessings are. Prepare to receive your *greater* blessing!

We should want God's favors. *"Lord, thou hast been favorable unto thy land: thou hast brought back the captivity of Jacob."* **Psalms 85:1** Isaac found favor with God in the midst of unpleasant circumstances. His favor will yield more than thirty or sixty fold. If you have the faith, you can receive a hundredfold blessing. God will actually start you out with a hundredfold blessing, but it is according to the faith that we have.

"If they obey and serve him, they shall spend their days in prosperity, and their years in pleasures." ***Job 36:11*** There are certain things we must do in order to experience God's choicest (a hundredfold) blessings. We must obey and serve Him.

"If ye abide in me, and my words abide in you, ye shall ask what you will, and it shall be done unto you." **John 15:7** We must abide in Him. The word "abide" implies that you "remain" in Him. You cannot walk in and out. Had Isaac went into Egypt against God's command, he would not have been abiding in Him. As long as you are the branch and remain on the vine, you will remain connected to the source that provides blessings. You have no power, if you leave the vine. The vine is your source of blessings. ***(John 15:1–2)***

My friend, remember this one thing, before your blessing comes, you will do a lot of things you do not want to do. But, *"Cast not away therefore your confidence, which hath great recompense of reward. For ye have need of patience, that, after ye have done the will of God, ye might receive the promise!"* **Hebrews 10:35–36**

In the Valley of . . .

Recognizing God's Faithfulness

THE BIBLE SAYS IN Psalms 119:90, "*Thy faithfulness is unto all generations: thou hast established the earth, and it abideth.*" Notice that this scripture is talking about God's faithfulness enduring to all. This includes you and me and everyone before and after us. He established the earth, the world, and it abides forever because of his faithfulness. One thing that I would like to point out about God's faithfulness is that He is *accessible, approachable, and dependable. "Confidence in an unfaithful man in the time of trouble is like a broken tooth and foot out of joint."* **Proverbs 25:19**. Do you know how bad a broken tooth or foot out of joint hurts? It is not a pleasant feeling. But you can always depend on God. His inspiration is greater than our desperation.

I just don't understand why people leave God. Perhaps it is okay for you to leave one church and go to another. Maybe that is God's will for you. But *it is never His will* for you to leave Him. I also do not understand why we as believers become so discouraged over nothing because the faithfulness of God is instantaneous and you can approach Him with your needs. Bad weather does not stop God. What people say does not delay God either. God's faithfulness means that *He will fulfill His promises*. He will do what He promised in His Word. The Bible says in the 10th chapter of the book of Hebrews verse 23, "*Hold fast to your confession...*"

Hold fast! Don't let go! Don't give up! Don't faint, because He is faithful that promised. God is faithful and He has always been faithful to me, always. And even when it did not seem like it, He has always been faithful to you. Do you believe that?

Just because God does not ring your doorbell when you want him to, doesn't mean that He is not faithful. He does not have to leave New York to get to where you are. So there is no time space between God and our problems. "*Lo, I am with you always until the end of the world.*" **Matthew 28:20** Did you realize that when you need to see a doctor or lawyer that you have to make an appointment? It is unheard of to see them directly. You just don't walk in and say, "Here I am!" Even after getting there, you must fill out endless amounts of paperwork, make co-pays and submit retainer fees. This is the process that you go through to get help from man. But you never have to go through that when you are dealing with God and operating in unwavering faith.

The more faith you have in God, the less you have to depend on the human process, and yes, this includes people.

> God is looking out for you when you are not looking out for yourself.

If it was not for the faithfulness of God, many of us would have already been destroyed. I know that there are some of us who believe that we are big and great; nevertheless, we really are nothing. Everyday you are decreasing, fading away, coming closer to your final moment on this Earth. I am not like I used to be. I don't walk like I used to. I don't get up like I used to and I can't eat the things I used to eat. These are sure signs that I am fading away. And, guess what friends? You are too! Some folks put cream and a whole lot of other stuff on their faces and use body enhancements to cover what is reality when they are actually standing in front of the mirror privately.

Reality stares back at you and allows you to realize that even with store-bought chemicals, you really do not feel any better. This feeling is a result of the glaring fact that enhanced beauty only produces momentary satisfaction. Be honest! Though we stand spiritually blemished at times, thank God that He remains faithful in meeting all of our needs, even without the cream that covers our physical defects.

There are not many people that you can depend on. If you are dependable, you will always do your best to help somebody else. Sometimes we are not dependable because there is a limit to what we can do. *Yet, there is never a limit to what God can do.* As a matter of fact, we should learn to take the limit off God and tell Him to have His way in our life. God will not violate our freedom to choose and think. ***Jeremiah 20:9***, the prophet became very discouraged because he was faced with the various problems of his divine calling.

Like many of us, he was facing some problems of preaching against the wickedness of the people at that time. But because of God's faithfulness, God touched him and he overcame his dilemma. Jeremiah boldly stated, "*I will not make mention of him, nor speak any more in his name.*" But because *God's inspiration was greater than his desperation, God's Word stood up causing Jeremiah to grip the fact that, it was just like fire shut up in his bones.* The Word of God forced him to unselfishly overcome himself. This was a point in his life where he accused God of deceiving him; but after God touched him, he began to praise the Lord, sing songs and continue proclaiming the Gospel that he had been purposed to preach.

> When God's inspiration becomes greater than our desperation, we rely solely on His faithfulness.

See, we can be down one moment and the next moment we are up saying, "Thank you Lord, for you were there all the time!" When You began to think about the faithfulness of God—*how you were healed, saved, delivered and set free, how he supplied you with money when you couldn't pay your rent or your bills, how you lived through various sickness even after being given up by the doctor,* it is easy for you to realize that it was *God's faithfulness that saw you through.*

Personally, I can think about some things I've gone through and it encourages and motivates me to go on. It is because of His faithfulness that we stand where we are on today. When I look back over my shoulder where God brought me from, I say, "*If it had not been for His faithfulness, where would I be?*" You should have the same testimony.

No one can fulfill God's promises but God—no one! The eldest son was complaining because of the prodigal son. The father killed the fattest calf and had all the jubilant music playing for him. And the eldest son said, "I am here all the time and you don't do that for me." The father replied, "All that I have is yours…" Now that is enough to tell me that all that God has is ours. ***Luke 15:11–32*** We do not have to read that any where else. How many times does God have to say something for us to take it seriously? I hear people say, "Can you find that again in the Bible?" You don't need to find it again. The Bible is the written Word. Jesus is the Living Word. And everything that the written Word says is manifested in the Living Word. And because He lives, we live also. Do you believe that?

Everything Isaiah prophesized about, *except Isaiah 65 and 17,* is fulfilled. *God's faithfulness endureth. It abideth forever.* He is faithful. When you call unto Him, He will answer. ***(Jeremiah 33:3)*** While you are thinking about it, making up in your mind that you need to pray, and yet speaking, He will say, "I am here!" Who wouldn't serve a God like this? *God has already provided the answer.*

Because God is faithful to us, we ought to be faithful to Him. Make up in your mind that on this year, you are going to be faithful to God. *Obey Him—Praise Him—Choose Him.* When you do this, you will experience His power abiding in your life.

Scriptures for Further Study: Psalms 119:90; Proverbs 25:19; Hebrews 10:23; Matthew 28:20; Jeremiah 20:9; Luke 15:11–32; Jeremiah 33:3

In the Valley of . . .
Walking, Working and Living by Faith

Am I Really Exercising Faith?

IT MATTERS NOT HOW much you say that you have faith. If you are not doing anything by your faith, then your faith is in vain.

The Bible says in ***Hebrew 11:6***, *"But without faith it is impossible to please him: for he that cometh to God must believe that he is, and that he is a rewarder of them that diligently seek him."* You can believe that there is a God, but your faith is not active until you start acting on what you believe. *The doing part is the fulfillment of the faith part.*

> There is a difference in believing in God and acting on what God says.

We can believe in God, but that is not faith. When you learn the Word, do what the Word says. This is why ***James 1:22*** says, *"But be doers of the word, and not hearers only."* It goes on to say that if you are a hearer only, you are deceiving yourself. You will not be blessed, unto you become a doer of the Word. But how can we become doers of the Word? A doer of the Word is simply responding to the Word through an act of obedience.

"For we walk by faith, not by sight:" ***2 Corinthians 5:7*** I walk by faith and not by what I see. Everything I see is tangible. Tan-

gible things are the elements of this physical world. In order to walk by faith, then I must walk according to the Word of God not by the limitations that this physical world has to offer. Here are some questions you should ask yourself. How can I walk by the Word of God if I do not know the word of God? So, then, you must study the Word of God—and do it diligently. Can I walk by the Word of God if I am not obedient to the God's Word? So, then you must choose to obey God's word. *God does not bless statements alone. He blesses commitments based on statements. God blesses what you do, not what you say.* You can say all kind of things, but if you do not do it, it does not mean anything. So then we walk by faith and not by sight.

A person living by faith is living better than anyone else. He may not have everything visible to the eye, but God is his Supplier. There is not one of us who has everything at their disposal. Nevertheless, I can guarantee you that God will never neglect your needs if you are living by faith. A person that is indoctrinated in faith and not religion does not worry about the cares of this life. If you worry about anything, your faith is weak. There is a difference between being worried and concerned. We should be concerned but never allow ourselves to fret and worry. Let the peace of God rule in your heart—by faith. Then, under any given circumstance and situation which may surface, your faith will see you through.

The Just Shall Live by Faith

Behold the proud, his soul is not upright in him; but the just shall live by his faith. **Habakkuk 2:4**

Your own faith can yield unto you a greater blessing from God than another person's faith. There are some people who do not mind selling out. They do not mind walking away from something now to get something better in the future." *For therein is the righteousness of God is revealed from faith to faith: as it is written,*

The just shall live by faith." **Romans 1:17** Paul looked back in the Old Testament and caught a glimpse of faith. "*As it is written, the just shall live by faith.*" It came by the way of a revelation of God. God put it there to let us know, if we are going to live for him, we must live by faith.

"*But that no one is justified by the law in the sight of* God *is evident: for, The just shall live by faith.*" **Galatians 3:11** There are people that talk, but do not do anything. A sinner cannot live by faith. In each verse it says that "*the just shall live by faith.*" If a sinner were living by faith, he would not be a sinner; he would be 'just.' A hypocrite cannot live by faith. If he were living by faith, he would not be a hypocrite. A churchgoer cannot live by faith—only the just, righteous and he who knows God.

"*Now the just shall live by faith: but if any man draw back, my soul shall have no pleasure in him.*" **Hebrews 10:38** When problems come up do not draw back. Face your problems head on and with confidence. Too many people draw back and then lose sight of faith. We have to learn about God. You cannot walk into a church and say I live by faith. Faith is a lifestyle that you live by. It is more than attending a worship service.

Faith yields to you what God has promised to give you. God looks on you and I and He sees that He has justified each of us through the blood of Jesus. "*Therefore being justified by faith, we have peace with God through our Lord Jesus Christ:*" **Romans 5:1** The blood of Jesus has justified you, not your good works, but your faith through Jesus. God knows all about you and me. He knows who we are, what we are about, how we think, and what we can become. God also knows what people think of you—but if you are living by faith, God will not allow destruction to come upon you.

Prove Your Own Faith

Some of our young people and even old are simply blessed on this earth because their family members are praying for them.

But that does not get a person into heaven. The earth is full of good things. Yet, the earth will pass and all the good things within it. The one thing that endures this temporary home is our faith in God. Everyone needs to exercise faith for themselves. Every time a new generation comes you recognize that that generation is weaker than the one before it. Each new generation is drifting farther away from God. Our young people are not really prepared for the next generation. Why? They are not living by faith. Yet, God is still working and He will always have a witness. But He is looking for faith. Someone to walk, work and live by it.

"What does it profit, my brethren, if someone says he has faith but does not have works? Can faith save him? So also faith by itself, if it does not have works, is dead. But someone will say, you have faith, and I have works. "*Show me your faith without your works, and I will show you my faith by my works.*" ***James 2:14, 17, 18*** God will never be guilty of anyone. He will do just what He said.

"No man shall be able to stand before you all the days of your life; as I was with Moses, so I will be with you. I will not leave you or forsake you." Joshua 1:5 The moment you see something failing, it is not of God. You may fail if you try to be like someone else. So, we need to stop trying to live like other folks. But if you are doing what He has called you to, He will not forsake you. God can't fail. If you fall, God will pick you up before you hit the ground! If God is for you, who can be against you? God has a purpose for us. God will bless you by teaching you how to be strong in the power of His might. There is nothing you can do in the church, and not reap what you sow. Not one prophet of God in the Bible failed when they were in His will. God is going to bless what I do, not what I say. And if I do His will, I have a right to be blessed. Do you agree? If so, then it is time to do more than talk—but make ready to walk, work and live by faith.

In the Valley of . . .

Going Further

And he went a little further, and fell on his face, and prayed, saying, O my Father, if it be possible, let this cup pass from me: nevertheless not as I will, but as thou wilt.

Matthew 26:39

THE GARDEN OF GETHSEMANE was a beautiful garden. So was the Garden of Eden. The difference between the two gardens was that Adam yielded to temptation in the Garden of Eden and Jesus was victorious over temptation in the Garden of Gethsemane. All of this because…He went a little further!

Are you falling short of your goals? Maybe it is because you have failed to go further when it is required of you to do so.

Jesus had a purpose in coming; He was sent here for a specific reason. You have a purpose for living and understand that you were born to fulfill a definite purpose. If you do not know your purpose, you are not really living, just existing. To fulfill your purpose, you must go a little further than you have already gone. To meet your goals, to realize your greatest potentials, you must go a little further.

Most of us really have not arrived. We have not made it to where God originally intended. Notice the agonizing struggle that Jesus faced during His earthly ministry. He had accomplished many good things, but He still needed to go further. What is clear in the scripture is that Jesus did not really want to die. Yet, in order to meet the goal and fulfill his mission, he had to press further. There are probably a number of things that you do not want to die to, but you must if you want to get further than where you are right now.

There comes a time in all of our lives when we need some help. Jesus had close friends. Peter was one of them. He asked his friends to pray with Him. Can you believe that? Even the Son of God asked for help. Have you ever needed help praying and no one could help you pray for just a little while? Many times in our lives we have friends that we desire to pray with us. Our friends can only go so far. We must accept that.

Jesus was having a struggle that has set an example for us who choose to follow Him. We will never reach our fullest potential without experiencing agony like Jesus did in the Garden of Gethsemane. Jesus even cried unto God. But it was not God's will to allow Jesus to stop from going further. If Jesus would have given up, we would be *"men most miserable."* We would have no way out. When Jesus died, He did not die for Himself—but He came for the sinners.

Jesus died for sin. While we were yet without strength, he died for the ungodly ***Romans 5:8***. God did not want his creation to be lost. Jesus was the ideal person, with the ideal solution, answer, and righteousness. *"He was made sin for us who knew no sin, that we may be made the righteousness of God in Him."* ***II Corinthians 5:21*** This is why we ought to make all the sacrifices we can for God. Had Jesus not gone a little further in the Garden of Gethsemane, we would not be free.

If you want to realize your goals, *you must go a little further*. If you want an answer to your prayer and be successful, *you must go a little further*. If you want to make it to the end and fulfill your purpose, *you must go a little further*.

Someone may have discouraged you, lied on you, and talked about you which caused you to stop pressing towards the mark.

Nevertheless, you must think for yourself and know what you are all about. Know where you are going. If you purchased a bus ticket to go to New York City and on your trip someone got on the bus and asked you to get off at Kansas City, why would you get off the bus? You paid to go to New York City.

People can cause you to lose your sense of direction. If you have made up your mind, *even if the struggle is agonizing*, you can make it. Jesus made it. It seemed like Jesus was going to be a loser, but the Power of God was demonstrated at the Cross. Had He stopped in the midst of His pain, had he stopped in the midst of criticism, had he stopped in the midst of temptation, God would have lost the battle. They denied Him, but He was able to endure the pain. You must be able to endure hardship as a good soldier. Do not give up. Do not stop. Keep digging. You are going to strike oil after awhile, but only if you *Go a little Further!*

In the Valley of . . .

Accepting the Anointing

DO YOU HAVE A burden on your shoulder? What about a yoke? A burden could be a financial one. It could be sickness or a health problem. If you have a yoke around your neck, a yoke will keep you yoked in. You are not going any place. You are not advancing in your life. Maybe it is not your time to advance. But even when it is your time, Satan will attempt to keep you yoked. *You have to break the yoke.* But you can only do it with the anointing.

Breakthrough

Did you know that you have to breakthrough from the natural? It is the natural that keeps you yoked down and the burdens upon your shoulder. Everything that we want God to do for us is spiritual and everything that God asks you to do in the Bible is for your victory. But you have to *break out* and *breakthrough.* You do not have to sin or be involved in gangs. You do not have to be involved in committing adultery or thievery. It is just from the idea that you are walking in the flesh and not honoring God that you will be yoked down. *You can go to work every day, be faithful to your family and never rise above your circumstances.* You know why, because you are yoked to the circumstances of life of the flesh and of the will.

Your faith is not being exercised to the point where you can get a complete breakthrough. The Bible says, "*...you shall know the truth, and the truth shall make you free.*" **John 8:32** Let me share this with you—only the truth that you know will make you free. ***Isaiah 10:27*** says, "*And it shall come to pass in that day that his burden shall be taken away from off thy shoulder and his yoke from off thy neck. And the yoke shall be destroyed because of the anointing.*" You can be so burdened down, that you do not even desire to live. Things can get so heavy until you just say, "I give up." And, that is the way the devil wants you to be—heavy, weighted down and desirous to give up.

Good News! Bad News!

***Luke* 4:18** reads, "*The spirit of the Lord is upon me, because He hath anointed me to preach the gospel to the poor.*" Good news! The gospel is good news and we would not need good news if there was not bad news. The bad news is that there are problems; the good news is that we have deliverance. The bad news is that we have burdens on our shoulders. The bad news is that some of us are yoked to circumstances that we cannot break loose from. Jesus said, "*Take my yoke upon you*" according to ***Matthew* 11:27, 28**, "and learn of me." He said my yoke is not a burden. "*My yoke is easy.*" Is that what is says? Read it for yourself! Now if the Bible is right, we do not have any business being yoked and burdened. Even though we might experience some insurmountable problems and go through some unpleasant circumstances, we have the power and anointing to destroy the yoke.

It's Already Done

Some people count it a sin not to come to a Bible study or prayer meeting and yet they are never delivered. I hope that you are not one of them. Now if you notice in the book of Isaiah it says, "*It shall come to pass.*" But if you notice in Luke 4:18 it says, "*he hath sent me...*" In other words, in the Old Testament this prophecy was yet to be fulfilled. In the New Testament, Jesus fulfilled it. Now, in this time, nothing else can happen. God will not do anything else. Jesus will not come again to bring deliverance. It is already here! Do you believe that? It's here! You are burdened down and yoked to circumstances. But, Jesus has already been sent to break that. Now, it is up to you and I to accept what have already been provided on our behalf.

Are You Under a Curse?

The reason why He had to bring good news is because there is so much bad news. All we talk about is bad news. Bad news! Who divorced who; who killed who; who did what; who you can't stand; who you don't want to speak to; who you don't want to see anymore; who you wish was dead. This is a reality. All you hear of is bad news and it is the works of Satan. Satan will do anything to help you lose consciousness of who you are in Christ. Did you catch that? If you are unconscious, you are unaware of your surroundings. You are blind to the aid that is standing right over you. So it is spiritually. When we lose our awareness of who we are in Christ, we believe that we are going to die; therefore we give up. When a person is carnal minded, then their mind is on the flesh. "*He that walks in the spirit will not fulfill the lust of the flesh.*" ***Galatians 5:16*** The Bible says in ***Galatians 3:13***, Jesus delivered us from the curse. A person that doesn't have Jesus is under a curse, the curse of the law. But those of us who are in Christ Jesus are free because Jesus was made a curse for each of us.

The curse is three-fold: *poverty, sickness and spiritual death.* This is a curse that no one can move but God. He bared and took our sin that we being dead to sin shall live unto righteousness.

"He was made sin for us who knew no sin that we might be made the righteousness of God in him," according to ***II Corinthians* 5:21**. But thank God, which causes us to triumph over all things! You know what the anointing really means? It is power to do the things that you cannot do. The anointing breaks the yoke of Satan. And, Satan acknowledges the anointing. The anointing is in the word of God. (Observation, interpretation and application) If you do not apply it, you cannot have it. You have to look beyond everything around you to be delivered. You have to push past your feelings and choose the power that is provided to us in the Word of God.

Unreliable Feelings

Do you realize that nothing could break the yoke off from the woman that had the issue of blood for twelve years but Jesus? ***Luke* 8:43** Only Jesus! She went to the doctor, spent everything she had and was still yoked down and had a burden on her shoulder. Perhaps, you can really relate to how she felt. If so, then you need the anointing. I want to encourage you to look for victory and deliverance in your life. Never look for emotion. Just because you may feel emotional does not mean that you are anointed. Salvation is not a feeling, it's a confession; it is a witness. The spirit, the Holy Ghost is a witness. Some people say, "Well, I went to church today and I didn't feel a thing." There are a whole lot of days that I come to church and do not feel anything, but I know that I have something. You do not have to work up a feeling. Just keep living, you are going to feel it, but that still does not mean you have deliverance.

The Power of the Anointing

The anointing will break the yoke. It will lift the burden. Jesus came to give us the victory. Now why should we be yoked down? Why should we have a burden on our shoulder? We cannot rest; we cannot do anything for God. We are always into something; we always have a problem on the east side and when we get it straightened out, we look around and it is over on the west side. We are always trying to overcome; always struggling in this life. We struggle until we are too old and cannot struggle no more. We struggle until we are dead and never see our victory! We do not have to. It does not have to be this way.

The anointing is here and available to lift us up out of our circumstances. Do not go another day without thanking God for the anointing in your life. Do not stress another minute without confessing the power over your circumstances. The power and anointing of God is available. All you have to do is thank Him for it. Believe you have it and walk in the victory that has been bought at the price of Jesus' blood on our behalf.

In the Valley of . . .

Receiving God's Grace

YOU MUST KNOW THAT God has you in His mind. The question is, "Do you have God in your mind?" Amos 3:3 states, "*Can two walk together, except they be in agreement?*" You cannot walk with God unless you agree with His Word and obey it. *And, we cannot obey God without walking by faith.* We should walk with God and give Him the glory. When we walk with God by Faith, we can expect God to give us everything that we have asked for. And, as a matter of fact, we should look for it. We should glorify God and tell Him, "Lord, because I walked upright, have done the right things and obeyed your Word, I am expecting for you to bless me indeed."

If you want God to do something for you that you cannot do for yourself, you must submit to the principles provided in His Word. There are a whole lot of things that we want and need done, which we cannot do for ourselves. For example, we cannot save ourselves, heal ourselves or give ourselves peace and joy. *And, many of us cannot stop doing things that we know is detrimental to our own lives. So, then, you agree that we need God.* Paul needed God. He needed help and deliverance. So, in the following scripture we find this experience of Paul:

> *For this thing I besought the Lord thrice, that it might depart from me. And he said unto me, My grace is sufficient for thee: for my strength is made perfect in weakness. Most gladly therefore will I rather glory in my infirmities, that the power of*

Christ may rest upon me. Therefore I take pleasure in infirmities, in reproaches, in necessities, in persecutions, in distresses for Christ's sake: for when I am weak, then am I strong.

II Corinthians 12:8–10

Paul prayed a prayer unto God because he was facing insurmountable circumstances. He was going through problems. Are you going through anything? Maybe you prayed and it seemed like the answer did not come. You knew that you walked upright before God and obeyed His Word. You recognized that you needed God and maybe even said to yourself, "but I prayed, I really prayed?" This is what Paul had done. He sought God for the problem that he was facing. He did not seek the Lord once, but three times. Obviously, this was a problem that was beyond his ability to solve. You may have circumstances that are also beyond your ability to solve. Know this; the Word of God is the answer to your problem.

Nobody wants to maintain pain that hurts. So what we do is wrestle and struggle with the circumstances of life. In Paul's case, notice the words "*depart from me*." This is because what he was going through was painful and no doubt, extremely burdensome. We want sickness to depart from us. We desire trouble to leave us. We do not want poverty to be near us. The Bible declares that pain shall be in the flesh of man and his soul shall moan. These are not pleasant experiences. So Paul sought God for his problem to depart from him. Did God answer his prayer? Not the way Paul desired for Him to. We have to accept the Will of God and understand that knowledge of who He is, becomes power to us. When you know God, no matter what you are going through, you will glorify Him. If you do not glorify Him, you will not only lose your Victory, but everything that surrounds a victorious life!

The Devil will tempt you to doubt God and over time, some of us will begin to give in to the Devil's lie. He will cause you to acknowledge that God did not hear your prayer. But allow me to share this with you my friends. God is God. He is concerned about the totality of man. However, He is more concerned about your character than He is your comfort. *We all want to be comfortable. We want to lie down without pain and have everything at our immediate disposal.* We want to walk in shoes that do not hurt, wear clothes that are not too tight. We want to drive cars that ride like a cushion. But there are going to be some uncomfortable circumstances to deal with as long as you are in the flesh. If you know God, when you seek Him, He is not going to answer you the way you expect Him to all the time, but rest assured, that His *Grace* will be sufficient regardless of the answer.

When God does not answer our prayer the way we thought he would, he always provides His grace to keep us in our weakest hour. There is no greater benefit than that of God's grace. It is more than sufficient to keep us. Paul was an anointed person. He had seen Paradise and had power with God. And, if God blesses us too much, His blessings will blow our minds. We then become super-humans and become better than anyone else. So then, we are given grace, so that the power of God may rest upon us and we do not become exalted above measure, even though we think we need something else.

You may find yourself wondering about your situation. The Devil will prompt you to consider, "if you are doing the right things and everything that God requires of you, then why are you going through all this?" Sometimes your response to the Devil may be in the form of you believing that God does not love you or you may convince yourself that you really deserve to be going through the hardship. Unfortunately, we make this mistake of fear and disbelief because normally we do not respond to the Devil based on the knowledge of God, but according to our emotions. It is vital in your walk with Christ to really learn and understand what righteousness consists of. It is not just a 'shout' in the camp.

Many times we are not 'shouting' (rejoicing and praising) based on what God is doing, but only because we feel good for the moment. Yet, we do not have the power to 'shout' out of our circumstances and we wonder constantly why we are in the same valley of defeat.

How can anyone who has not been faithful expect for God to bless them? Shouting is not what brings blessings. Faithfulness and obedience brings God's blessings. God accepts no substitution for obedience to His Word.

God's grace is yours. It is free. It is a benefit. You can be thankful for whatever circumstances you are facing, especially when you understand God's grace. There is not a person who under all circumstances will have everything to be just right. You will never live in a situation where everything is always just right. There are some things that work to our benefit because they cause us to get closer to God. If you be honest with yourself and look back over your life, you will begin to thank God for not giving you everything you thought you wanted.

When you get to the point where you understand God, and are mature, accepting whatever he brings your way, you are ready to be blessed. When you are weak, God will supply your strength. When you trust God, you are not losing out. Even though you may be cast down, you are still a winner. Things around you will oftentimes fade away, but you have not failed as long as you remain in God. I submit to you that instead of complaining, we must learn to glory in our infirmities and God will give us the strength we need. The more you talk about how strong you are in God, the stronger you will be. Start now accepting the grace of God. It is more than sufficient to sustain you in your time of need.

> We must learn to glory in our infirmities

In the Valley of . . .

Being a Pushover

But now we are delivered from the law, that being dead wherein we were held; that we should serve in the newness of spirit, and not in the oldness of the letter. **Romans 7:6**

But if ye be led of the spirit, ye are not under the law. **Galatians 5:18**

NOTICE THAT PAUL SAID, "*Now we are delivered from the law.*" This means *now*—not tomorrow, but while you are reading this. How can you be delivered from the law? According to **Romans 8:2**, "*the law of the spirit of Christ Jesus hath made you free from the law of sin and death.*" Although this scripture shares with us that the Spirit of Christ has released unto us freedom, the questions of manifestation yet remains. When are we able to see it? My friends, manifestation occurs the moment you believe what you have read. Do you believe that you are free? Do you agree that you have been delivered? The key is *Belief*.

When you are under the conviction that causes you to believe without doubt, it becomes easy to tell the Devil and the enemies that surround you or your circumstance that you are delivered. The Devil does not honor "Hallelujah" or "Thank You Lord" unless those sayings are accompanied by Word of God. When Jesus was in the wilderness in ***Matthew 4th Chapter***, He did not go around singing jubilant songs of "Hallelujah." He did not lift his hands and say, "Praise the Lord Saints"! Jesus, who was the Word, quoted the Word—and this is what we as the believer must do.

You do not have to know the whole Bible, but that which you do know, believe and apply it to your everyday life. You must learn to take things personal when it comes to the Devil attacking you. Remember, you are by yourself at midnight going through. You are by yourself in the dungeon. When you have a Doctor's visit, he writes a prescription for you. It is not for everybody, not even those in your household, but you alone. So, then, you must take the Word of God as a prescription from God for your personal victory.

> You must take the Word of God as a prescription from God for your personal victory.

If no one else takes it, take it for yourself and use it.

Galatians 3:13 shows us that the law is embedded with a curse. This curse is threefold: *poverty, sickness and spiritual death.* Therefore, since you are delivered from the curse of the law, then you are delivered from *poverty, sickness and spiritual death.* Do you believe that? ***Deuteronomy 28:15–65*** explains in detail about the curse of the law. It is very important for you to know that you must do more than attend church and say, "hallelujah" during the time of high spiritual emotions. Many of us are without understanding why we even do certain things in church. Perhaps it is because we have seen someone else doing it. Or maybe we heard that it was the "thing to do" in order to be noticed by God. Whatever the case, in reality these persons do not really experience true victory over the enemy. Let me remind you of a couple of things. Your victory is not in being a member of a church. Your victory is not even in the influential people you know. *Your vic-*

tory is in knowing Jesus (the Living Word) completely through His sufferings and the power of His resurrection. ***Philippians 3:10***

Most of our efforts in this life are living to make the world a better place. There is really nothing wrong with this effort. However, we should not leave a better world and go to a burning Hell. Do you agree? It is not worth it. We need to spend time trying to make ourselves better. We do a lot of things trying to make ourselves good, not realizing that we are only making ourselves "good for nothing" if we are not saved. The Bible says that "*the wages of sin is death*." ***Romans 6:23*** This is the paycheck persons receive for living a sinful life—it is death. It does not make sense to play church because God's Church is not playing. There are many now in the valley of indecisiveness. They cannot decide whether or not they want to live for God. For the scripture says, "*The fool hath said in his heart that there is no God*." ***Psalms 14:1*** Doing well is alright, but there is a more excellent way found in Jesus Christ that is always better.

The Devil is a pushover. He is a coward. *But, he will try his best to convince you that you are a pushover and a coward*. He has already been defeated, but he will try to turn that around and make you think that you are defeated. He will deal with your mind and imagination constantly and encourage you to react to his actions. You must remember that every action of the Devil should be reacted with the Word of God in our lives. Unfortunately, most of us do not know that and those who do know it, rarely exercise it. You have to learn to let the Devil know that *you are not a pushover*. You do not have to be a fool. And this does not mean that you are better than anyone else. It just means that you have good sense. You are not a religious person—just spiritual and spiritually, you have been given authority over the Devil's actions. A religious person does not have spiritual authority.

> *For Christ is not entered into the holy places made with hands, which are the figures of the true; but into heaven itself, now to appear in the presence of God for us:* **Hebrews 9:24**

What does this mean for us? When you get into the Word and are abiding in Jesus, you are in the presence of God. Many of us have fallen from this commitment. We are not like we used to be. We don't *pray* or *love* like we used to. God will give us space to repent—whatever you do, take advantage of it. It is not because we are good that we are left here, but it is because of God's mercy. You cannot manipulate God. He does not forget anything. Right now, you have an opportunity to get right with God. The Bible declares in ***John 8:34***, "*Whosoever committeth sin is the servant of sin.*" You cannot serve two masters. You cannot come to church, sing in the choir or serve on the deacon board and then leave and serve the Devil. You must love one and hate the other. It does not matter what you say, if you are serving the Devil, than you hate God and vice versa.

Learn to honor God's Word. You honor the Word by speaking, believing and trusting in it when the Enemy attacks you.

> *And they overcame him by the blood of the Lamb, and by the word of their testimony;* ***Revelations 12:11***

Not by doctrine or church rules, *but by the Blood of Jesus Christ*. Your denomination is irrelevant when it comes to your victory over the Devil. The question is, do you know Jesus? You are only responsible for what God has done for you. Can you accept that? A lot of times we try to defend ourselves. Yet, the strength that we think we have is not good enough for this spiritual fight and in reality it is useless. Accept what Jesus has done on the Cross. Believe in it and remind the Devil that he is already defeated and that you are not a pushover, but more than a conqueror through Christ Jesus.

We allow things to take us from the reality of what God is all about. We learn Theology and we refuse knee-ology!

The word, "Now" is so important in the scripture. We must understand its full meaning. It means exactly what it says, and that is, at this present moment. Not even a minute later. "Now" you are delivered. Not based on how you feel, or what thoughts come to mind. You must know what the scripture says—believe it and stick to it. You don't have any other time than "now." 'Now' is all you have. God is always in the present tense. Right now He's working. You must accept His Word—*now*.

Section Four

Preparing for His Return

In the Valley of . . .

Living in the Last Days

And it shall come to pass in the last days, saith God, I will pour out of my Spirit upon all flesh: and your sons and your daughters shall prophesy, and your young men shall see visions, and your old men shall dream dreams: And on my servants and on my handmaidens I will pour out in those days of my Spirit: and they shall prophesy. **Acts 2:17–18**

ACCORDING TO THE BIBLE, we are living in the last days, not the last day. The last days began when Jesus was born. We are 2000 years into the human history of the last days. Joel prophesied in 2:28–32, in his time that God would pour out of His Spirit upon all flesh. So, again, the last days are from the time Jesus was born until the Second Coming of Christ. Many of the prophecies have been fulfilled. Joel prophesied in 835 B.C. Peter picked this up centuries after that prophesy was told. So, then we learn from that that every Word of God is true. There are some prophesies that have not been fulfilled. What the Bible is teaching us is that there is no hereafter for Human Government or for a person to receive Salvation. We are in the last days. Take advantage of the golden opportunity to receive

> Take advantage of the golden opportunity to receive God's plan of Salvation and to live right.

God's plan of Salvation and to live right. Human history is rapidly bringing us to a close of these last days.

Many events that God spoke of through His prophets are beginning to come to pass. We see things now that we have never seen before. People are acting now like they have never acted before. We live in a technology-driven society where men do not have to do anything but push a button. So this takes away men's potential that God has given him. It makes men lazy. They have it now where you can order your sermon. Someone else will print your message. But what this does for us is that it makes our mind become lazy. And, as you probably already know, when your mind is lazy, you as a person are lazy. It causes us to stop studying the Bible for ourselves. Yet, the Bible has declared, "study to show thyself approved unto God." It causes us to stop meditating. Yet, the Bible has declared, "let the words of my mouth and the meditation of my heart be acceptable in thy sight, O Lord, my strength and redeemer." It causes us to stop praying and laying before God. Yet, the Bible has declared in Luke 18:1, "that men ought to always pray and not faint."

Because of these things, I question how we can receive a revelation from God. Every time we witness and come before God's people, we need a fresh revelation from God.

The pulpit is not the place to get even with people. It is the place that determines the direction of the Church. No one can give you the direction of the church but God. It does not matter how good a theologian you are. You can not lead people spiritually without God's revelation. Every one that reads this book will interpret it differently because everyone's needs are different. God knows what we need. It is not good to feed the God's flock—leftovers. It is not good to try to excite God's people. Jesus said that the flesh profits nothing. If a Medical Doctor is going to help the natural body, he has to first hurt it. If the Servant of God is going to help the spiritual body, they must give it what it needs first. And, sometimes what it needs—hurts.

There is a difference between calling and choosing. You can find it in the Bible. Moses was called eighty years prior to him being chosen. If you read Acts 9, you will see that Paul was called. However, he was not chosen until the thirteenth chapter of Acts which was fifteen years later. Many are called but only a few are chosen. Why is this? I believe it is because between calling and choosing there is preparation. And there are so many persons who do not survive the preparation process. This preparation stage allows us to get grounded and stabilized so that we do not embarrass the Holy Ghost. If you are in the flesh, God cannot use you.

God will never send you out until you are prepared. God requires faithfulness. God cannot create faithfulness in you. You must supply faithfulness. "If you be willing and obedient, ye shall eat the good of the land." God will not make you obey. Obedience is something that you have to do. You must make up in your mind that what the Bible says is true and that you are going to obey it.

In the last days, according to 2 Peter 3:3, the scripture declares that mockers will come. Persons will criticize you. Covenant breakers and doubters. They will say, "where is the coming of God." When is God coming? My brothers and sisters, be encouraged, God is long-suffering. Everyone has a part in the ministry of God. There are no un-important people. There is no insignificant ministry. Everyone is not supposed to be doing what you are doing. A horse is not supposed to give milk. You are not supposed to ride a cow. A rooster does not lay eggs and a hen does not crow.

We must be careful that we do not walk in the counsel of the ungodly. When the time comes for God to fulfill His Word there is nothing that can stop Him. Let every man be a lie, but God true. The devil is seeking to cause the Church to deviate and leave its first love. We are living in an age of deception. Be careful—you might get tricked. Whosoever will, let him come....

Isaiah 26:2 talks about the righteous nation who "keepeth the truth until the end." No one but the righteous will enter in. Only He who holds on to God shall be sustained. Behold, I stand at the door and knock...

In the Valley of . . .

Striving To Enter In!

JOHN 15:7 SAYS, "*IF you abide in me, and my words abide in you, you shall ask what you will...*" The verse goes on to say, "*and it shall be done unto you.*" Or, we could say, it shall be done for you; done on your behalf. Let us evaluate that word "will" some more. Your will is in your soul. Your soul consists of your sensibility, *your thoughts, your imagination and will.* So then, when the Bible speaks of asking anything or receiving anything according to your will, *you have got to have that in your soul and not just in your mouth.* Do you remember when the lepers came to Jesus saying if thou will thou can make me clean? And Jesus replied and said, "*I will that thou be clean.*" **Mark 1:40–42** Jesus' *will* connected to the man's *will* that had the leprosy. See, when it is in your spirit and in your will and in your soul, the Word of God connects with you and to you. It is not just in your mouth. We can learn to say these kinds of things, but it must connect with your spirit in order for you to get blessed.

"Strive to Remain Focused"

Many times, the reason why we do not get blessed is because we do not pray long enough for our blessing. We do not pray long enough to put ourselves in-tune with the Spirit of God. "*He that hungers and thirst after righteousness shall be filled.*" **Matthew 5:6** We all have to learn how to communicate and articulate God's language and put ourselves into God. *We want God to come into* *us but then God wants us to put ourselves into Him*. That is why he said, *"If you abide in me and my Word abide in you."* If you stay there, remain there, remain attached and continue there, you will be blessed. *Do not let circumstances separate you from God*. Do not let problems, which includes, people, places and things cause you to deviate or change your focus. You see, what we want from God, it comes from the inside. The Kingdom of God is not over there. It is not over here. It is not in the desert, nor somewhere else, the Kingdom of God is within you because the Word of God is within you. ***Luke 17:21***

Revelations 3:20a says, *"Behold I stand at the door."* In other words, He is standing at our will. But, the knob is on the inside! That means you have to let Him in. Furthermore, faith is the only thing that can open the door. This daily walk is not a religious, denomination or church thing—it is a Christianity thing! It is a "Holy" thing. *You can go to church all your life and be lost*. If you want to be blessed you have got to learn how to be blessed. Let me share this with you. I really do not know how to work my cellular phone. I just know how to receive calls. There are a lot of benefits that came with my phone and I do not use any of them. To be honest, I do not need them. I just need to know how to call home to my wife and to call whoever I want to call. I do not need a picture on there! I do not need all of that, but it is on there. Similarly, you have benefits that you do not receive because you do not know how to work it. You do not know how to make it work. You have a will; you got to get into it. It has got to abide in you; you have to feel it. You have got to want it so bad until you do like Jacob. I'm not going to let you go—you're going to bless me! ***Genesis 32: 24–32*** You have to get in the right place with God. You have to know within yourself, "yes, I have it already."

"Now faith is the substance of things hoped for," according to ***Hebrews 11:1***. *"The substance of things hoped for, the evidence of things not seen."* I like that scripture because faith is the evidence.

I do not see it but faith says I have it. *Faith knows it's there.* Did you catch that? Faith moves God. Faith says, "Yes God, You've got to give it to him." You cannot come in and get on your knees and say, "Hey, here I am God. It is me again." You have not been to church, studied the Word, or prayed for some time now. Let me tell you, God cannot bless part-time lovers. If you are a "Sunday-go-to-meetin" saint, you are just a part-time lover. If you do not study your Bible, you are just a part-time lover. If you do not pray, you are a part-time lover. You do not just jump up and say, "I love God." And, if you love God, you will do what God said. And, if you really want to do what God said, you will learn to love God so you can do what He said.

The Straight Gate

> *And He went through the cities and villages, teaching, and journeying toward Jerusalem. Then said one unto Him, "Lord, are there few that be saved"? And He said unto them, "Strive to enter in at the strait gate."* **Luke 13:22–24**

Look, he said, *strive to enter in at the straight gate.* For many, you will seek to enter in and shall not be able. *Strive. Fight the good fight of faith. Agonize. Put forth effort.* Strive against pressure, against the works of the devil. The pressure that is upon you and upon society and upon this world and upon all of us, individually and collectively, is the pressure from sin. There was no pressure in the Garden of Eden until Adam and Eve transgressed the law of God. You have pressure in your family because somebody in there acts a fool. We have pressure in our community because we have someone going around breaking in houses. So sin creates a problem.

Getting Rid of the Weight

"Strive to enter in at the straight gate." That means you can not carry any weight. Whenever you go to the airport, you must go through security. And, only one can go through that security gate at a time. You have to unload, pull off your shoes and watch, and all kinds of other things off. You have to take some weight off. And, if you go through there and have something on that should not be on you, then the buzzer goes off, and they say, "Back up!" You cannot have a belt and barely suspenders. So, when I go through there I just say, "You want me to pull off my clothes?" If this is your rule, I'll obey it. You cannot even take your money through there. It is too straight for your account. So Jesus said *strive* because he knew that it would be difficult. You are not just going to get saved and come to church and go to Sunday School and learn John 3:16 or Matthew 7:7, "ask and it shall be given." If you are walking low, you are going to straighten up and fly right to get through the straight gate. Titles, gifts and callings are without repentance. Your denomination and church fellowship will never get you through the straight gate. It will be a single line and every man will give an account of his own deeds.

Hebrews 12:1 records *"Lay aside every weight and sin." Now weight will not keep you from going through the straight gate. But sin will and weight will hinder you.* Some people will weigh you down. The devil uses people to weigh you down. We have church folks that weigh down other folks. They do not pray. They tell you all their problems and they are not trying to do anything to solve their own problems. So then, you cannot be weak and help other folks that are weak. A weak wife cannot help a weak husband. *"Finally, my brethren, be strong in the Lord and in the power of His might."* ***Ephesians 6:10*** The reason why David could outdo Goliath is because he was strong, he knew more. He knew how to fight. So you see, to strive means—I have to agonize and put forth effort.

You are not fighting against flesh and blood but you're fighting against principalities and powers. ***Ephesians* 6:12** You are fighting against something that you cannot see but can feel. You cannot see it but it can attack you and take everything you have. You cannot see it but it can come in your house and divide your family; it can cause you to lose all your money. You are fighting against a devil that does not love you. He does not want you to go through the straight gate, because there is another scripture in the Bible that says, "*Wide is the gate that leads to destruction and many will go therein.*" **Matthew 7:13** Jesus also said, "*except you take up your cross and follow me daily, you cannot be my disciple.*" ***Luke* 9:23** And, then the other word in there it says except you deny yourself and this is where we lose.

It is difficult for us to deny ourselves the things that we are used to, the things that we love, the things that we want, and the things that make us happy. Everything that makes you happy is not good for you. Everything that is *good to you is not good for you.* So, you have got to let go of your friends because when you get to the gate, no friend can walk beside you. This is why we have to live holy and righteous and sanctify our own self and live for God by faith. There are some people in hell because they let other folks cause them to go to hell. You cannot afford to let anybody cause you to go hell. That does not mean you have to treat other people wrong. You do everything right for your family and friends, but you can never take them through the straight gate with you. When I leave here, when God calls me home, I cannot take anybody.

"The Works of Righteousness"

Only the works that I have done and it has to be the works of righteousness will stand before God. Then, some said to Jesus, *"Lord didn't we cast out devils in your name? Didn't we witness in your name? Didn't we feed the poor in your name? And Jesus said, depart from me you workers of iniquity, you did all of this in my name, but I don't even know you."* ***Matthew* 7:22–24** The reason I do not know you is I am looking at my book here. I know you went to church and you conducted prayer meetings. You sang in the choir. You did all of these things. You even built churches, you had big congregations, and you had small congregations. But I do not know you. I am looking here at the book. I have two books here; I only see your name in one book. That is the book that spells your name going through the wide gate.

God has a recording secretary. He has you and He knows your deeds. He has me and He knows my deeds. He is a God of no respect for persons. My witness is in heaven and my record is up on high. ***Job 16:19*** Nobody in here knows my record except God. Nobody in here, individually, knows your record except God because He knows your motives and thoughts, and He is acquainted with all your ways. The only way that God could judge you faithfully and justly is by knowing you. See you can fool some folks sometimes, but you cannot fool God at any time. He knows your tomorrow. He knows your down setting, your uprising, your thoughts afar off. And it is because of God's mercy that we are not consumed. ***Lamentations 3:22*** He is longsuffering. Some people say, "I wonder why God let me live so long?" It is because He's longsuffering. He's longsuffering and the reason why God is longsuffering is because it is not His will that any man should perish. ***II Peter 3:9*** The reason why He is longsuffering is because He is giving you a chance to repent.

Holiness or Hell

The Bible says Be ye holy because your heavenly father is holy. Be righteous because your heavenly father is righteous. You are going to have to strive to get through the straight gate. You cannot pay your way in; you cannot talk your way in. But while you are down here in your right mind you can live your way in. I am sorry to tell Brother Bishop he will not be able to go through the straight gate just because he is a bishop. I am sorry to tell brother Pastor you will not be able to go through the straight gate just because you are a pastor. I am sorry to tell bother deacon you will not be able to go through the straight gate just because you are the head deacon. I am sorry to tell the choir president, you will not be able to go through the straight gate just because you are the choir president. I am sorry to tell the first lady she will not be able to go just because she is the first lady. You have got to be holy.

Section Five

Q&A on Finances and Marriage

In the Valley of . . .

The Principles and Promises of Giving

Question #1: Why is it important to pay tithes?

Pastor Dunn: Well, I believe that it is important to pay tithes because it is the Biblical principle for wealth and prosperity. All tithes belong to God and we are just stewards of the monetary blessings He give. God made the world and the fullness thereof and they that dwell therein. Even the king's heart is in the hands of the Lord. We really do not own anything, but God blesses us to be stewards. ***Leviticus 27:30*** reads, *"and all the tithes of the land, whether of the sea of the land or of the fruit of the tree is the Lord's, it is holy unto the Lord."*

Malachi chapter 3:8–10 *reads "Will a man rob God yet ye have robbed me but ye say wherein have we robbed thee in tithes and offerings. Ye are cursed with a curse for ye have robbed me even this whole nation. Bring ye all the tithes into the storehouse that there may be meat in mine house and prove me now herewith saith the Lord of Host if I will not open you the windows of Heaven and pour you out a blessing that there shall not be room enough to receive it."*

Pastor Dunn: God let's us have 90% of our income or our earnings and He only asks for 10%. When you give God 10%, he strategically doubles the 90% in some instances.

***Matthew* 23:23** *reads "Woe unto you, scribes and Pharisees these hypocrites! for ye pay tithes of mint and anise and cumin, and have omitted the weightier matters of the law, judgment, mercy, and faith: these ought ye to have done, and not to leave the other undone."*

Pastor Dunn: What Jesus is saying to the scribes and to the Pharisees is that you should have good morals, but also you should pay your tithes.

***Question #2:* We have had some real emergencies which have caused us to use our credit cards more than we wanted to. We want to know if this is a lack of faith using them in these instances, even though we didn't have any other avenues for finance. What is God's answer to that, Pastor?**

Pastor Dunn: Well, I do not think it is a lack of faith, I think it is a lack of financial planning. In many cases, we do not live within our means. Just because we are paying tithes and blessing God with a portion of our income, does not mean that we should spend foolishly what is left over.

***Hebrews* 10:23** reads: "*Let us hold fast the profession of our faith without wavering; (for he is faithful that promised;)*"

Pastor Dunn: God is faithful that promised and God promised to supply all of our needs which you will see in the next scripture.

***Philippians* 4:19** reads: "*But God shall supply all your need according to his riches in glory by Christ Jesus.*"

Pastor Dunn: I think that we should limit ourselves to our needs in some cases, when we are not able to do everything that we want. There is time and season for everything and God will bless us if we use wisdom and follow the biblical principles that God has laid down for wealth and prosperity. It is not an overnight trip: the road of success is always under construction.

***Question #3:* How can we trust God and not waiver on what He has promised especially when it seems like we are financially struggling to just make ends meet?**

Pastor Dunn: When a person really obeys God and lives within their means, there is never a struggle because the yoke of God is easy. It is when we live beyond our means that we get into trouble.

James 1:6, 8 reads, "*But let him ask in faith, nothing wavering. For he that wavereth is like a wave of the sea driven with the wind and tossed. A double minded man is unstable in all his ways .*"

Pastor Dunn: We should never be double minded if we want God to bless us. We do not have to struggle, but we must focus and have faith in God. We must hold to our conviction in God as it relates to everything that we do. It must be done according to the Word of God. The Word cannot lie. His promises are sure. God wants us to depend on Him. In the times in which we live, you will not always have the income or the resources from jobs or whatever means that you are planning your livelihood. But God is our resource and He will never, never, run out.

***Question #4:* What principle or formula does the Bible set out or give us on being debt-free? And I will go further to ask, what are the step by step ways of giving our way out of debt?**

Pastor Dunn: God will bless you, but we have to use common sense. If you want to be debt free, you cannot really have everything that you see. You cannot yield to temptation. Not only that, you must not build high credit. High credit is what causes you not to be debt free. If you pay cash for everything then you are debt-free, right?

Philippians 4:11–12 reads, "*Not that I speak in respect of want: for I have learned, in whatsoever state I am, therewith to be content. I* *know both how to abased and I know how to abound: every where and in all things I am instructed both to be full and to be hungry, both to abound and to suffer need.*"

You cannot always be full, meaning that you have an abundance of everything. There comes a time in your life where you learn how to walk by the principles of God's Word, which are wisdom, knowledge and understanding. He will bless you to be debt-free. But there will come a time before you become debt-free that you might "want" or be in a state of "wanting." You will have to deny yourself satisfaction now, so that you can enjoy financial freedom later. In other words, I deny myself today so that I can live better tomorrow.

Question #5: Is debt a sin?

Pastor Dunn: Debt is not a sin; it is a weight. We will find that in ***Hebrews 12:1*** which reads, "*Wherefore seeing we also are compassed about with so great a cloud of witnesses, let us lay aside every weight, and the sin which doth so easily beset us, and let us run with patience the race that is set before us.*"

Pastor Dunn: From the natural aspect, when we lay aside debt, we lay aside financial burden and weight. Since debt is a weight, ("How am I going to pay this?" or, "I don't have enough money this week"), put God first and He will help lift some of that weight off you through wisdom, understanding, and knowledge. As a matter of fact, it is such a weight that some nights you cannot even sleep and many days you do not answer a ringing telephone. Too much debt is unhealthy. ***Proverbs 10:22***, "*The blessing of God it maketh rich and addeth no sorrow.*" Now, the blessings of God make one rich, but many times we are not waiting for God blessings, we are blessing ourselves.

Question #6: What are the consequences of not giving sacrificially?

Pastor Dunn: Well, I believe that if we read ***Romans 12:1, 2***, it will answer that. How can we be devoted to God, give God our lives and He ask each of us to give our body sacrificially and not give our resources sacrificially? I don't think that we can give ourselves individually to God sacrificially without giving our substance. ***Romans 12:1, 2***: "*I beseech you therefore, brethren, by the mercies of God, that ye present your bodies a living sacrifice, holy, acceptable unto God, which is your reasonable service. And be not conformed to this world but be ye transformed by the renewing of your mind, that ye may prove what is that good, and acceptable, and perfect will of God.*"

Pastor Dunn: It is good to give sacrificially to God; but, I also believe that our mind has to be transformed before doing so. I also think that we cannot be conformed to this world and give to God sacrificially. Not our means, resources, and ourselves, because our minds are too focused on satisfying the lust of the flesh.

Question #7: I do not attend church, but I pay tithes and donate my offerings to a successful ministry. What expectations should I have of God in harvest time as I continue to sow these seeds?

Pastor Dunn: Well, as you sow you should expect a harvest. But at the same time, what profits a man to gain the world and lose his soul. A person cannot expect to go to heaven or be saved, without being in some church under some ministry that is preaching the full Gospel. Let us go to the Word of God for that, ***Psalm 62:5***. "My *soul, wait thou only upon God; for my expectations is from him.*" ***Jeremiah 3:15*** reads, "*And I will give you pastors according to mine heart, which shall feed you with knowledge and* *understanding.*" This is one reason that you should attend church. It is easy when you are blessed, or when you are able or when you are under conviction to send your tithing. But, God also wants you and your service, so God has a church just for you because he said, "*I will give you pastors according to his own heart.*"

Romans 10:13, 14 and 17, "*For whosoever shall call upon the name of the Lord shall be saved. How then shall they call on him in whom they have not believed? and how shall they believe in him of whom they have not heard? and how shall they hear without a preacher? So, then, faith cometh by hearing, and hearing by the word of God.*" You should pay your tithes. It is a blessing to pay your tithes. The rich man in the ***16th chapter of Luke*** had as much money as any rich man could have. But when he died, he lifted his eyes up in hell and of all the money that he had while on earth, he could not even get a drop of water. What a sad situation to be in. His money was good on earth, but he chose not to be a good steward of it in that he refused to help the poor. Don't allow greed to govern your heart; give back to God and you will never be in a state of lack.

Question #8: Why is the love of money considered evil when money is essential in building God's kingdom and needed in order to financially assist in spreading the word of God?

Pastor Dunn: You should love nothing or anyone greater than God. ***Deuteronomy 6:4*** reads: "*Hear O Israel: the Lord our God is one Lord. And these words, which I command thee this day, shall be in thine heart.*" We should love the Lord our God with all of our heart, soul and strength. Money is not evil. In fact, throughout the New Testament, Jesus talked about money and even sent Peter to get money from the mouth of the fish in order to pay His taxes. However, in many instances, we allow the love of money to overtake us and that is when it becomes evil. It is the abundant love of anything that is evil, to include the love of your family or material goods, more than God. Evil is attached because we find ourselves doing whatever it takes to acquire and maintain what we have "fallen in love" with. ***Matthew* 22: 37–39**: *"Jesus said unto him, Thou shalt love the Lord thy God with all thy heart and with all thy soul, and with all thy mind. This is the first and great commandment. And the second is like unto it, Thou shalt love thou neighbor as thyself."*

***I Timothy* 6:10, 17** *"For the love of money is the root of all evil: which while some coveted after, they have erred from the faith, and pierced themselves through with many sorrows. Charge them that are rich in this world, that they be not high minded, nor trust in uncertain riches, but in the living God, who giveth us richly all things to enjoy."* If you love money, you will trust money. Whatever you love, that is what you will put your trust in unconsciously. Maybe we feel like we could solve problems by becoming rich. We say things like, "if I had the money, and my son, daughter, wife, or myself ever got into any serious trouble, I would have enough money to obtain proper help." Sounds great, but what happens when you are in a situation that money cannot solve? You cannot buy life in the midst of death, even if you have enough money to pay the best doctors. Have you ever realized that? Well, you are not the only one. Let's go back to our rich man in the Bible. Yes, the rich man lived sumptuously. As you know, everyday his life was probably full of servants waiting on him. But he did not have enough money to keep him from dying. When God said this night your soul shall be required of you, his wealth and riches were null and void?

***Question* #9: Are we supposed to pay tithes from just our earned income, our job, or from all the money that we receive such as gifts and income tax? Perhaps, some of us receive money from a 401K. What is the plan for that? Or, alimony, child support, do we pay our tithes from that Pastor? Can you explain that to us?**

Pastor Dunn: You pay tithes on the first fruit of your increase—no matter what form it comes in. I know people have asked, about paying tithes on a welfare check or other sources of income that do not come from a job, per se. Clearly, my answer is that if the items mentioned above serve as your source of income, then yes, you owe God a check equal to 10% of whatever income you are bring in! If you work on a job, that is your source of income. If you are getting an income tax check and you have already paid tithes on that, then I would not say that you have to pay tithes on it. But, if you are getting above and beyond what you paid tithes on before you invested, then sure, you should pay tithes on it. ***Proverbs* 3:9** says: "*Honour the Lord with thy substance and with the first fruits of all thine increase. So shall thy barns be filled with plenty, and thy presses shall burst out with new wine.*"

If I invest twenty thousand dollars and three months later or three years later that twenty thousand dollars generated back to me twenty thousand and six hundred dollars, well I already paid tithes on the twenty thousand. It is my duty to sow God tithes on the six hundred. Isn't that simple? You will get more money by obeying God completely. Some theologians play this down. God is an honest and just God. He is not out to rob anyone; we are just robbing ourselves. God gives us a privilege to prove Him. God tells you that if you do not believe my word, try me and prove me. He says I will open up the windows of Heaven and pour out more than what you are able to receive. ***Malachi* 3:8–10.**

The Devil will get into your spirit and creep into your mind and show you what you could do if you just held on to that money or even the gifts God has placed inside of you. **Matthew 10:8** reads: "*Heal the sick, cleanse the lepers, raise the dead, cast out devils: freely have ye received, freely give.*"

When you freely receive God's resources, whether it is the gift to cast out devils, or the gift to speak a kind word to a hurting sister or brother, freely give. Give according to the Word of God, according to the scripture, and then you can ask God what you will. The Bible says that if you abide in Him and His words abide in you, ask what you will, it shall be done unto you. But, if you are not giving according to God's principles, then how can you demand God or ask God to bless you? You do the math.

In the Valley of . . .

Love and Marriage

***Question #1:* When I met my wife, we were unsaved. I have since accepted the Lord in my life. However my wife is still doing the same old things and it is causing so much stress in our marriage. How can I lead her to Christ when she still wants to go to the nightclubs?**

Pastor Dunn: I believe ***Jeremiah 31:3*** will give us the answer. "*The Lord hath appeared of old unto me, saying Yea, I have loved thee with an everlasting love: therefore with love and kindness have I drawn thee.*" Kindness conveys loyalty, faithfulness and truthfulness to your spouse. And although you may be saved, and she may not be saved, you yet have an obligation to each other because you are married. I believe through love and kindness, you can draw a sinner to Christ with prayer and patience—that is our duty.

***Question #2:* We have three children and we are surviving off one income. My husband doesn't want me to work, but I think I should so that we are not struggling financially. What should we do?**

Pastor Dunn: I believe that you should obey your husband and if you do, God will make a way. Children need their parents at home. ***Philippians 4:19*** reads as follows: "*But my God shall supply all your need according to His riches and glory by Christ Jesus.*" God will supply all your needs because every child needs their mother or father or both at home to discipline them or keep them under control until they come to the age of accountability where they can make their own decisions.

Psalm 34:10 reads as follows: "*The young lions do lack, and suffer hunger: but they that seek the Lord shall not want any good thing.*" If we trust in the Lord, God will provide for us.

Question #3: My husband and I have children and do not wish to have any more. Does the Bible teach against birth control?

Pastor Dunn: Well, I believe that God has a purpose for each of us and that we should seek God for his will, no matter how many children you may have. God is able to sustain you through the process of bringing up your children and I believe the Word will answer that in ***I Timothy 5:14, Genesis 1:28 and Psalm 127:3–5***.

I Timothy 5:14, states that: "*I will therefore that the younger woman marry, bare children, guide the house, give none occasion to the adversary to speak reproachfully.*" If you notice this verse does not put a limit on how many children you should bear.

Genesis 1:28 "*And God blessed them, and God said unto them, Be fruitful, and multiply, and replenish the earth, and subdue it: and have dominion over the fish of the sea, and over the fowl of the air, and over every living thing that moveth upon the earth.*" It's God's plan that in marriage, we should have children. God will bless you. It is God's plan that we should fill the earth with children and with everything that God has put upon the earth to reproduce itself. If you're married, and you notice, I keep saying "*married*" because it is a sin to have a family outside of marriage, God has instituted marriage to bring forth children and to have a family.

Psalm 127:3–5 "*Lo, children are an heritage of the Lord: and the fruit of the womb is His reward. As arrows are in the hand of a* *mighty man; so are children of the youth. Happy is the man that has his quiver full of them: they shall not be ashamed, but they shall speak with the enemies in the gate.*" I believe the Word has spoken and if we believe the Word and obey the Word, I am sure that God will make a way and give you a revelation, guiding you into what you should do.

Question #4: I am having a hard time forgiving my husband as he has been unfaithful to me numerous times. I love him very much and I know my anger is wearing on him because I am so hurt by this. How can I forgive and forget so that we can move on? What advise can you give him also about being unfaithful?

Pastor Dunn: Well, I believe a husband should be faithful to his wife and if there is a disagreement between the two of you in your relationship, then you should seek God to help you overcome any animosity, resentment or unforgiving spirit that is presently growing inside of you. God's Word has the final authority for what we need to know when it comes to living peaceful and a life together in unity.

Mark 11:24–26 says, "*Therefore I say unto you, What things so ever ye desire, when you pray, believe that ye receive them and ye should have them. And when you stand praying forgive, if ye have ought against any: that your Father also which is in Heaven may forgive you your trespasses. But if you do not forgive, neither will your Father which is in Heaven forgive your trespasses.*"

To maintain a good relationship in your marriage or even between friends, it is important that you always exemplify and exhibit a forgiving spirit. So, reference Romans 12: 9, 10, and 21.

***Romans* 12:9**, says "*Let love be without dissimulation. Abhor that which is evil; cleave to that which is good. Be kindly affectioned one to another with brotherly love; in honor preferring one another;*

Not slothful in business; fervent in spirit; serving the Lord;" Serving the Lord means that when a problem comes between you and another person, if you want to maintain your relationship with God, you must have a forgiving spirit. We must therefore forgive, so that we are forgiven, just as God did for us by sending His Son Jesus into the world. Therefore, if you don't forgive, the Father will not forgive you. Remember, forgiveness is always having peace with God in your heart.

Question #5: **My wife and I are saved; we drink sociably, and listen to rhythm and blues music occasionally. Is this detrimental to our salvation?**

Pastor Dunn: Definitely! Because you cannot love God and the world. ***I John 2:15–17*** reads as follows: "*Love not the world, neither the things that are in the world. If any man love the world, the love of the Father is not in him. For all that is in the world, the lust of the flesh and the lust of the eyes, and the pride of life, is not of the Father, but is of the world. And the world passeth away, and the lust thereof: but he that doeth the will of God abideth forever.*" We must remember that God does not listen to rock-n-roll; you must remember that God is a Holy God and you cannot love the things of the world and please God simultaneously. II Corinthians 5:17 will indicate to you that once you receive Christ that you are no longer the same person that you used to be. "*Therefore if any man be in Christ, he is a new creature, old things are passed away behold all things are become new.*" What you did before you received Christ or before you repented of your sins, can no longer be routine and acceptable behavior—*forget the old things*. When God cleans you up, He forgives you for your sins. So that means that you should not keep or have a desire to keep doing it. You need to pray about that.

Question #6: I have a high sex drive, but my wife does not. What can I do so that I am not complaining about sex?

Pastor Dunn: Well, I believe that although you are married you should control your passions or sex drive. After all, you have to consider that your wife is human and I believe the Word will answer that. ***Ephesians 5:22***: *"Wives submit yourselves unto your own husband as unto the Lord."* Looking at the situation, it is easy to say that the wife should submit herself to her husband and to his desires. But, also, the husband must be temporal in all things and not over do it. We should consider each other. And if we do that, our love will remain strong. Sometimes, we have to deny ourselves and not seek to fulfill our desires of the flesh, to include our sexual passions. **Colossians 3:18 says,** *"Wives submit yourselves unto your own husbands as it is fit in the Lord."* A wife should submit herself to her husband, but her husband should have a profound understanding that they are both human.

Question #7: **We are trying to raise our children according to Biblical standards. What does the Bible say about discipline?**

Pastor Dunn: Well, I think we should go to Proverbs 22:6, 15 and I believe that God gives us a program and level of principles on how to bring up our children. God would not ask us to have children just to let them go wild. I think that we should discipline our children without abuse and use methods of discipline *that will not hurt them*—abuse is wrong. **Proverbs 22:6** *"Train up a child in the way he should go: and when he is old, he will not depart from it."* I don't think you can train a child unless every now and then you spank him/her. There is nothing wrong with that; however, there is something wrong with harsh abuse. We should use a level of spanking that the child can take without leaving any marks or any thing that will hurt them and we should learn where to spank. ***Proverbs 22:15*** *"Foolishness is bound in the heart of a child; but the rod of correction shall drive it far from him."* I believe that we should use the rod of correction. This doesn't mean a piece of iron or stick. The rod is not talking about that, but what it's really talking about is that you should do what is necessary without abusing the child to drive the foolishness out of their heart because they do not have the level or ability to think like an adult.

Question #8: **I am currently working in the ministry. It is obvious that God has given me a great gift. It is difficult talking to my husband about it because he is busy with his duties as a deacon. How can I discuss with him that I have a calling from God without looking like I am taking away from him?**

Pastor Dunn: Well, if you both are in the ministry, there should be no separation because God is a God of peace and not confusion. I think two people in the ministry should be able to work together although their gifts might be different. ***Psalm 133:1*** *"Behold, how good and how pleasant it is for brethren to dwell together in unity!"* There is a place for everyone in the ministry.

Question #9: **My boyfriend and I have lived together for a couple of years and we have just gotten saved. We have not discussed marriage; however, we have many financial ties. What is the right thing to do now as we are so financially linked or dependent on each other?**

Pastor Dunn: Well, if you both are saved, the right thing to do is to get married and start a family together. It is a sin to live in a house together, boyfriend and girlfriend. Therefore, God has instituted marriage to make it legal and more financially stable.

Proverbs 18:22 says "*Whoso findeth a wife findeth a good thing, and obtaineth favour of the Lord.*" The favor of the Lord is manifested when you get married. You do not have any favors living together unmarried from God, because you are not husband and wife. ***I Timothy* 5:14** reads: "*I will therefore that the younger woman marry, bare children, guide the house, give none occasion to the adversary to speak reproachfully.*" There is that word again—that you should get *married* and bare children and guide the house. There is no reason why we should continue in what we are doing if it is sinful. We will not be blessed if we continue to live in our sinful ways. ***Hebrews* 13:4** reads "*Marriage is honorable in all, and the bed undefiled: but whoremongers and adulterers God will judge.*" I think that scripture speaks for itself. If marriage is honorable, then shacking or living together is dishonorable. It speaks for itself.

Question #10: I work outside the home and my husband is a stay at home dad—we have been told that we are "outside" of our roles in the family—is this true?

Pastor Dunn: I would not say that this is necessarily true. If two people agree that the wife should work, and the husband should stay at home, if there is a harmonious relationship between those two I believe that it works. We do not understand the relationship between husband and wife in some things. I would not say yes, I would not say no; I would say, however, it depends on your decision. ***Amos* 3:3** "*Can two walk together, except they be agreed.*" So, if you agree that a husband should stay at home, the wife should work and you are yet walking together in love fulfilling your marriage responsibility, then that is your decision. I believe that God will honor that.

Give the Gift of

IN THE VALLEY OF DECISION

INSIGHTS TO SUSTAIN YOUR FAITH

to Your Friends and Colleagues

CHECK YOUR LEADING BOOKSTORE OR ORDER HERE

❑ **YES**, I want _____ copies of ***In the Valley of Decision*** at $12.95 each, plus $4.95 shipping per book. Canadian orders must be accompanied by a postal money order in U.S. funds. Allow 15 days for delivery.

❑ **YES**, I am interested in having Roosevelt Dunn speak or give a seminar to my company, association, school, or organization. Please send information.

My check or money order for $__________ is enclosed.

Please charge my: ❑ Visa ❑ MasterCard

Organization ____

Address ____

City/State/Zip ____

Phone________________________ Email ____________________________

Card # ____

Exp. Date_____________ Signature ______________________________

Please make your check payable and return to:

Decision Time Publishing

P.O. Box 5011 • Colorado Springs, CO 80931

Call your credit card order toll-free to: (877) 772-9938

Fax: (719) 457-0740

www.israelitecogic.org www.decisiontimetv.org